Get Real!
MONEY

7 Get the Money
You Want in Just
Minutes a Day

JIM GUARINO

NewDiscovery™
NASHVILLE

Published by New Discovery NASHVILLE
A division of New Discovery Media Corporation
615-333-9843
www.NewDiscovery.com

First Edition 2005
Printed in the United States of America
10 09 08 07 06 05   1 2 3 4 5 6 7 8 9 10

ISBN 0-9746829-9-3

New Discovery books are available at special quantity discounts for bulk purchases for sales promotions, premiums, fund-raising, or educational use. Special books, or excerpts, can also be created to fit specific needs. For details, please e-mail a request to: SpecialMarkets@NewDiscovery.com.

Cover design by George Foster: www.fostercover.com
Interior design and production by The Roberts Group:
  www.editorialservice.com

Get Real!, 7 Minutes, Money Expert, 7 Minute Secret, American Financial Education Network, Cash Flow Safety Zone, Five Master Money Strategies, $1,000,000 Investment Account Strategy, Diamond Mining System, Business Blueprint, Financial IQ, Real Solutions—Real Fast, New Normal, Loan Schedule Strategy, Strategic Alliance Strategy, Diamond Clues, New Discovery, its marks, and logos are trademarks of New Discovery Media Corporation.

A portion of the profits of this book will go toward providing food and care for disadvantaged children throughout the world.

Dedicated to the thousands of students, customers, and business clients who over the past twenty-five years have been committed to Get Real!

To your continued success,
Jim Guarino

TABLE OF CONTENTS

ACKNOWLEDGMENTS

Special thanks to my wonderful wife Jennifer for helping me "get real" and teaching me the importance of love and relationship. Anna, Lea, and Joey, thank you for each being the special person you are and giving me the privilege of being your dad. Thank you to Mrs. Marie Guarino, my mother, for your encouragement and eternal optimism.

Thanks to the team of experts and associates who have also worked hard with me in the creation of this book.

CHAPTER 1

The Get Real! Philosophy

IMAGINE HAVING THE MONEY TO DO the things you really want in life—spending more time with your loved ones; having more time and money for recreation and travel; being able to comfortably fund charitable giving, your retirement savings, and your children's or grandchildren's education. Yes, it's going to take *real* money, and that's why I wrote this book. In today's paycheck-to-paycheck existence, it's almost impossible for people to get ahead. Everybody's trying their best, but most struggle just to break even. People need another solution—one that they can easily manage and which, over time, will produce the results they want—and that's exactly what you will get in this book. In these pages is the *real solution to get real money.*

Most of us are too busy today to be able to drop everything we are doing to learn and apply new ways of making, keeping, and investing money. We need easy-to-understand, straightforward solutions, telling us exactly what to do in order to get the results we want, as fast as we can. I call these straightforward solutions "*Get Real! Strategies*™." *Get Real! Money Strategies*™ are 21st century solutions to the common money challenges most people face today. This book is the result of thousands of hours of study, research, and intense application in the area of money, and it is written to save you the time and effort.

First, I want to congratulate you for *being* real and telling yourself it's okay to have money. That's the first step to *Get Real! Money*. The reality is, everybody needs money, and most people spend an entire lifetime working for money, so, I'm glad you've concluded that it's okay to get real *with* money and discover how to *Get Real! Money*. This book will be exciting for you and can change your life. The process begins with a new vantage point, a new way of seeing yourself, a new way of operating in relationship to the world around you. I call this *The Get Real! Philosophy*™.

Today we're living in unprecedented times of constant change. By the time we get used to something, it changes—again. The world of money has changed dramatically over the last fifty years, and today we need *new* strategies for dealing with it. *The Get Real! Philosophy* is the basis of this book and forms a solid foundation by which you can better navigate the real world you live in. The *Get Real! Philosophy* may at first seem like just plain common sense; yet many times a simple idea will have a powerful impact. *The Get Real! Philosophy* will pay you huge returns when you put it to work. Once you know *The Get Real! Philosophy*, you will be ready to *Get Real! Money*.

Get Real! #1: Play to win

Get real with yourself, get real with others, and get real with the world around you. That's it; there's nothing else to it—call it what it is. Wishful thinking on your part is not going to improve your current financial situation, and the sooner you get real, the sooner you'll position yourself for becoming effective in the new world of money.

Smart people acknowledge reality and avoid unreality. Hoping, wishing, and praying, by themselves, are not *winning* financial strategies. Believing things aren't what they are, or that somehow they will become what you want them to be, isn't living in reality. It's much easier to change the things we can change, and accept the things we can't.

Smart living is coming to a realization and acceptance of the playing fields on which we live and participate. Each field has rules to play by, and if we don't play by the rules, we're thrown out of the game. One playing field is our work life—the place we work, the people we work with, and the rules that govern that environment. You have to show up for work at a predetermined time and place as well as perform certain functions. Another playing field is our personal relationships. This field has a different set of rules, depending if you're single, married, or have a family. Every field has its own set of rules.

One key to success is to learn the rules, play by the rules, and *play to win*. Life is very much a game that takes determination and discipline and needs a playbook of concrete strategies. The problem with the playing field of money is that most of us were taught rules that don't work any longer, or perhaps never did. Our parents did their best, but they didn't know the *real* rules or secrets of the game in order to teach us.

What you hold in your hands is the playbook of concrete strategies for the real playing field of money in the 21st century.

Get Real! #2: Get real *with* money

If you want to get *real* money, start by getting real *with* money. America has a huge financial mess on its hands, and we all need to roll up our sleeves and get busy fixing it. We're living in an unprecedented day and age of prosperity, but there are dark clouds on the horizon. It's time to get real with the facts:

- Personal bankruptcies, credit card debt, and property foreclosures are at an all-time high.
- Social Security is out of cash, according to the General Accounting Office (the auditing arm of Congress).
- Personal saving is at an all-time low.
- More and more people are living in poverty.
- Quality jobs are harder to come by.
- The national debt is at an all-time high.
- The average worker works three hours out of every eight hours to pay taxes.
- Fewer and fewer people have retirement plans in place.
- The baby boom generation, born between 1946 and 1964 (more than 80 million people), is planning to retire soon, and the majority don't have the resources to do so.

What's going on, and how can this be happening? Isn't America the wealthiest nation in the world, with the highest standard of living?

I understand that you may or may not be one of the millions with financial woes—up to your ears in debt or expecting a Social Security check from a government that may not deliver—but millions of Americans are. Either way, we all need a wake-up call, because what's happening will affect everyone. How do you think millions of baby-boomer retirees who have little to no income are going to survive, especially since we're living longer? Where is the money going to come from? Generally speaking, there are two possibilities: raise taxes or pull the plug—literally. Today's American financial picture is the direct result of fifty years of broken financial ideas that are about to blow up in the faces of millions of people who are not prepared. Don't let that be you! To *Get Real! Money*, you have to first get real *with* money.

This book is the solution for the financially unprepared.

Get Real! #3: Compress time

You're in a hurry. You don't have time to go back to school to learn what you need to know about money. Your time is valuable, limited, and precious. Get real about the fact that you are growing older by the minute and that you need easy-to-understand and simple-to-implement solutions. You need to learn how to *compress time* and get done in three years what will take the undisciplined, the long-ranger, the know-it-all, or the financially clueless person years to do.

This book offers solutions to help you accomplish in a few years what will take others a lifetime, if ever, to accomplish.

Get Real! #4: Eliminate risk

Learning how to make real money, how to invest it properly, and how to use money wisely isn't risky—despite what some might have told you. Developing wealth is risk-free, as you'll learn in this book. Learning how money really works and what to do with your money isn't risky—it's smart.

Here's what I consider risky: driving my car on roads with people who are talking on cell phones, drinking coffee, and steering with one knee. Or, how about believing an employer will appreciate your effort and hard work, keep you gainfully employed, and help you retire; or waiting for the government to find a solution for a broken Social Security system; or waiting to inherit money; or eating fast foods—these are the real risks in life!

Learning how to *Get Real! Money* is risk-free. Doing what it takes to become financially successful doesn't require going out on a limb.

This book is your risk-free formula for financial success.

Get Real! #5: Act on opportunities

There has never been a more opportune time in recorded civilization to achieve financial success, as well as success in our personal lives, our health, or our careers. We simply have more opportunities, more choices, and more information than any other generation in recorded history—and we're living longer. This means we have more opportunity to figure it out and get it right. You have the capability to learn how money works and exactly what to do to get more of it.

This book is hope for your financial situation today and in the future.

Get Real! #6: Be positive—yes, you CAN do it, too

Keep this in mind: If someone else can achieve financial success, you can, too. Whatever you see other people accomplish, once you put your mind to it and make the decision, you can do it, too.

It still amazes me that some people will say that money isn't important, yet they work an average of three hours a day to pay the government before they themselves get paid. Many work an average of forty plus hours a week for an entire lifetime to bring home a check, spend it, then go back and do it over again, sweating it out on the money treadmill. I've found that some people have actually convinced themselves that they enjoy the rat race for money. You may have heard it said before, "Money isn't the most important thing in life, but it's high in priority along with food, oxygen, and water!"

Money is incredibly important to most people in America, whether they admit it or not, because people want more of what money can do *for* them. *More money equals having more choices.* Financial safety and security is a *choice.* Spending quality time with the ones you love is a *choice.* Giving time and money to help others is a *choice.* Having time and money to better care for ourselves is a *choice.* What we do for work, when we work, how much we work, and who we work with are all *choices.* Having time and money to do the things we want to do doesn't just take money—it takes a choice, and that choice takes *real money!*

Your financial success is a choice you have to make. By choosing to use just one new strategy over the next few days, you can learn how to *Get Real! Money*. But remember, it's *your* choice. In this book, I will show you, step by step, what you need to know to bring *real* money into your life so you can develop *permanent financial security* in just seven minutes a day. You will acquire the *financial intelligence* your parents and schools didn't give you, and you'll do it in just seven minutes a day. I'll make it easy for you and cut through the clutter of books written about money, and by the time you finish this book, you'll have a higher *Financial IQ*™ than 99 percent of the rest of America, in just seven minutes a day. I will launch you on an exciting journey with what I call the 7 *Minute Secret*™. But remember, ultimately, it's your choice. Yes, you CAN do it, too.

Get Real! #7: Take seven minutes a day

I first learned the secret behind the 7 *Minute Secret* when I was ten years old. My mentor at the time was Mr. Favreau, my guitar teacher. He showed me one idea that has transformed my life forever. I'll never forget our conversation during my first guitar lesson. He said, "Jimmy, you want to become a great guitar player, don't you?"

"Yes, of course," I said.

My teacher said, "There is one secret, and one secret only, you'll need to know for this to happen. *You must practice seven minutes a day, every day, no days off, and then you will reach your goal.*"

I said to myself, "No problem; I've got this licked. I can easily do seven minutes a day, every day, no days off." Here's what I discovered in the process. I committed myself to applying myself seven minutes a day, every day, no days off, but what my mentor didn't tell me was what would happen. *After the seven minutes were up—I kept on going.* The first seven minutes were the hardest part. My fingers hurt, and I wanted to go outside and play with my friends. But after just a few minutes, something special started to happen. I worked past the hard part, *my attention was activated,* and I just kept practicing, every day, no days off. What my teacher knew was that I had an attention span that would last thirty to forty minutes and that if he could get me through the first seven minutes, and if I did it every day, no days off, the rest would take care of itself—and it did. *I developed the habit* of daily applying myself to my goal, and I went on to become an excellent guitar player. I have since used the 7 *Minute Secret* in other areas of my life where I wanted to accomplish goals—and you can use the 7 *Minute Secret* to discover how to *Get Real! Money* just as I have.

By the time I was fifteen in (1973), I had already started using the 7 *Minute Secret* to learn how to work for myself. By nineteen, I owned an entertainment café as well as a recording studio, which doubled as a music training facility. That same year, using the 7 *Minute Secret,* I also started my first retirement account, and by age twenty-one, I was investing in real estate. As I continued in business and investing, having proven the power of applying the 7 *Minute Secret* in my own life, I began speaking on the topic at the age of thiry-two and training others to do the same by using the *Get Real! Money Strategies*—for seven minutes a day.

Today, I am founder and president of the *American Financial Education Network*, whose mission is to provide quality resources, tools, and education for personal and business success. Over the past fifteen years I've had the privilege of training more than 100,000 smart people to make solid financial decisions, to better manage money, to get out of debt, to start and operate a business, to expand an existing business, to safely invest money, to buy real estate with little to no money or credit, to make additional income beyond their day jobs, to achieve long-term permanent financial security, to adapt to this changing world and make new career decisions, and most importantly, to maintain the *inner drive to take action* with what they've learned.

Individuals, families, business owners, corporate officers, and employees from all walks of life, people just like you, have attended my education seminars called *Get Real! Money Seminars*™. My students are from various backgrounds and professions—blue-collar workers, truckers, contractors, white-collar workers, engineers, nurses, teachers, financial professionals such as CPAs, bankers, real estate agents, insurance agents, financial advisors, Fortune 500 executives, lawyers, physicians, highly successful entrepreneurs, struggling business owners, professional real estate investors, builders and developers, musicians, artists, full-time moms and dads. People ranging from the unemployed to senior corporate executives, from the flat broke to multimillionaires—you name it, I've trained them.

I've discovered that millions of Americans—from all walks of life, whether lower or upper income, whether they have little education or are highly educated, men and women aged 18 to 89—have something in common: They are hungry for quality financial education to better their lives. They want to learn how to *generate more money*, how to achieve *permanent financial security*, and how to *safely invest*, so that some day they won't have to work for money—*money will work for them*. I've worked with thousands of hard-working people who have lost jobs after years of commitment and loyalty to an employer, and I've helped others who are in search of alternatives to their traditional careers or business endeavors. More than ever, people are thirsty for new ideas, strategies, and knowledge on how to earn a living and have a fulfilling lifestyle in today's ever-changing *knowledge economy*. You may find yourself wanting these same things, and you may be wondering if *Get Real! Money* will work for you.

If you want to improve your finances no matter what

situation you find yourself in, *Get Real! Money* will work for you. If you are financially upside-down or your credit is in shambles—that's okay, *Get Real! Money* will work for you. If you are living paycheck to paycheck, sick and tired of being sick and tired, and ready to move on to the next level—*Get Real! Money* will work for you. If you are doing quite well yet have underlying insecurities because of your dependence on only one form of income or if your career is unfulfilling and offers little to no real retirement—*Get Real! Money* will work for you. If you are in business, already working as long and hard as you can, but all your eggs are in one basket—*Get Real! Money* will work for you. I promise I will not waste your time. These proven principles have worked for people for hundreds of years, and they will work for you, too.

By committing to the 7 *Minute Secret* to begin with, for just the next few days, you will learn more about money than you have learned in your lifetime. Unfortunate but true, most of us can wrap up in one sentence what we were taught about money: *Figure out a way to make it by working for someone else, try not to spend it all, try to save some, and keep trying to make more of it. Try, try, try.* There's obviously more to it for the person who desires *financial safety and security* and does not want to be left behind paycheck to paycheck.

But please don't be fooled—you don't need more detailed *information* about money. What you need is a crystal clear, straightforward *game plan* for real long-term financial success, and I have condensed what you *really* need to know in one easy-to-use place—this book.

Most important, you've got to do what I teach you, not merely think about it or talk about it. My goal is not only to help you see a bigger and brighter picture of opportunity, but also to help you take action and create momentum by using the 7 *Minute Secret.* This book is the right road map at the right time—for you.

The question is: are you ready to get real *with* money, and are you willing to *invest* seven minutes a day, every day, to improve your financial life?

Excellent! *Now* you are truly ready to *Get Real! Money.*

The Get Real! Philosophy™

Get Real #1: Play to win.
Get Real #2: Get real with money.
Get Real #3: Compress time.
Get Real #4: Eliminate risk.
Get Real #5: Act on opportunities.
Get Real #6: Be positive—yes, you CAN do it, too.
Get Real #7: Take seven minutes a day.

CHAPTER 2

Find the Money That Makes You Rich

EVERYBODY, EVERYWHERE, WANTS TO KNOW: "Where's the money, and what is the one magic formula for success?" Yes, there is a secret—and it eludes people everywhere, every day. This is it.

Get Real!

Successful people don't know it all or have it all together—they just find out what they need to know and who can help them; then they take action!

In reality, there are strategies, resources, and people you don't know yet. Successful people know how to find and access the right people and best resources to get what they want. No one cares more about *your* personal finances than you. It's time to get real and believe that you are just as capable as anyone to *find* the right strategy, *find* the right people, and *find* the right resources you need in order to experience

13

financial success. No matter what anyone has told you before, you do have what it takes. But first, you'll need to know and understand *The Five Master Money Strategies*™ covered in this book and have access to the best resources available.

I chose to provide you with additional information on our Web site, www.GetRealMoney.com, for several reasons. First, I want to give you overwhelming value for your investment as a new student of mine. Secondly, I want you to have access to other necessary resources and the right people you'll need over time to reach your goals.

You no longer have the option of doing things the old way, unless you want the same results you're already getting. In the 20th century, a sound financial strategy meant getting a good education and a good job. Isn't that exactly what your parents taught you? Work for a stable company that will give you reasonable hours, a couple of weeks' vacation, health insurance, and a permanent retirement income. What a great plan. And it worked for our parents and grandparents.

But today—sorry—the *playing field has changed*, and that's exactly why you need a brand new financial strategy that works in today's world. You can no longer expect to find a company to provide permanent employment and a comfortable living. Employers today are competing in an entirely different environment and must remain flexible, able to move quickly and decisively in order to remain competitive. To cut costs and increase profitability, the first option a corporation will consider is to cut human resources. Employees are an expensive and expendable liability that can be eliminated overnight, leaving whoever is left to continue doing the work. If you're thirty years old, you've probably been there at least once—and maybe three times if you're in your sixties. This is the reality of our day and age. And it's safe to assume that this trend is permanent.

Get Real!
The playing field and our economy have permanently changed

The industrialized America of the last century was dependent on a large domestic workforce to lower costs. Today American manufacturers have learned to lower their costs by relying on machines and overseas labor. Today we are living in a knowledge-based economy with a different set of rules. Either you get it and play by the rules, or you don't. And if you don't, you will be swallowed alive during the next ten to twenty years. Either you prepare yourself for financial independence or you'll lose the game and take your place among the *have-nots*. And it's no surprise that the gap between the *haves* and the *have-nots* is rapidly widening.

In the old days, it sufficed to get through high school, maybe go to college, and educate oneself just enough to bring a technical skill or ability to the marketplace. But today the marketplace is constantly changing, growing, and shifting under our feet. Much of today's knowledge will be obsolete within a few years. In this economy, you can be fifty years old and told you're unemployable because you're too old. It's just not like it used to be. It's hard to accept, but you must.

Get Real!
Become dedicated to ongoing education in your personal and professional life

To become financially successful today, you must be dedicated to gaining specialized knowledge about money. That's why this book will be one of your most important tools for turning up your financial fire. *Get Real! Money* is specialized, focused education that teaches the key elements you'll need to remain financially viable throughout the 21st century. One of the fastest ways to access the specialized knowledge needed to improve your life is by reading.

I was fortunate to have a father who dedicated his career as a college professor to helping people learn how to read. As a child, all I knew was that my dad taught teachers how to teach reading. That sure sounded b-o-r-i-n-g to me at the time. As a kid, I really didn't enjoy reading. It was a chore that had to be done, and I did it as little as possible.

Get Real!
Self-educate yourself a minimum of seven minutes a day

Years later in my late teens, I remember sitting at a diner with a friend having a cup of coffee. My friend pulled out a book and started reading. Feeling a little put off, I asked him what he was doing, and I'll never forget what he said that day, because it changed me forever. "I'm reading to enhance my mind," my friend said. "I bring something to read wherever I go." My heart sank inside my chest as I thought to myself, "I wish I had a desire to read." Remember, it was ingrained in me that reading was a key to success, yet I read only what I had to in order to get by. I felt resentment at first, then jealousy, then—liberation. I've long believed that if someone else could do something, then I could, too.

That moment with my friend—me sipping a cup of coffee and he reading a book—was a major turning point in my life. I decided then and there that I too would bring something with me to read wherever I went. Even if it was just two or three pages, even if for just *seven minutes a day*, I began reading information that magnetically directed me to where I wanted to go in my life. I have since become a voracious reader, and it is not unusual for me to be reading five books simultaneously. I have read or reviewed thousands of books and articles of nonfiction that were relevant to my personal and professional life, including personal finance, investing, real estate, business, marketing, psychology, marriage, parenting, spirituality, healthy living, and physical fitness. I've invested more than 15,000 hours reading and researching, and I have concluded beyond a doubt that the information we gain by reading, if we choose well, can improve any aspect of our lives.

I also listen to CDs and audiotapes in my car whenever I drive. I call it my university on wheels. I attend educational seminars to stay informed in my areas of interest. I'm a huge believer in focused adult education where I can quickly receive information that can immediately be used to get results. Over the last fifteen years I've become an expert at leading these adult education programs myself, having conducted hundreds of them throughout the United States. (Please visit www.GetRealMoney.com for details.)

Over the years I have learned the ultimate strategy from all my research and application. Successful people don't *need* to know it all. For years I've hired advisors, mentors, coaches, and professionals in order to get where I want to go as quickly and as painlessly as possible. People who have already been where you are can show you exactly what to do, as well as what not to do. Given the choice, I prefer to learn from other people's mistakes rather than my own. Today, I function as a leader, educator, advisor, mentor, and coach. Individuals and businesses throughout the United States hire me for my experience, expertise, and specialized knowledge—all of which are a direct result of using the 7 *Minute Secret.*

Get Real!

Acquiring specialized knowledge in the area of money is necessary for the person who wants more of it

Reading, listening to educational audio, attending live events, and surrounding yourself with experts are powerful tools that will motivate, educate, and inspire you to further achievement and success. As you begin using the *Five Master Money Strategies*, you'll become aware of something that's been waiting to be strengthened—seven minutes a day. I call this your money muscles.

Money muscles are the thoughts and beliefs you hold about money. *Money is a mind game.* To get real money, you need to know what you truly believe about money, because money begins in the mind—then it's in the hands. Your mind is your money muscle, and it's time to put it to work to give you the results you want.

Get Real!
Take charge!

Get real, put your foot down, and take control—take total control. Make the commitment to take charge and live your life to its fullest potential. Too many people buy into the idea that once they receive the high school or college diploma, they've finished the education process. However, learning never really ends. Lifelong learning is the *realization* that you don't know it all.

The more you pay attention to personal self-development, the more you'll assure eventual success. This always results in having more of the life you *choose* to have. The person who decides it's not important to continue to grow, especially in today's world, is in big trouble. You can only *Get Real! Money* by taking full ownership of your life. Now is the time to strengthen your money muscles and take charge by applying *Get Real! Strategies.*

Most people don't want to be left behind financially, in relationships, or in personal satisfaction. Today you can't afford to sit back and hope everything will take care of itself. You must have the skills to meet the demands of the new century. We live in a much different world than we did just twenty-five years ago.

Today we expect free time, physical health and vitality, and quality relationships; we want money to do the things we want to do, and we want security. And by the way, most people would prefer not to have to work if they didn't have to. Previous ways of finding security through family, community, or national pride have become harder and harder to find. We may live thousands of miles away from our closest family member. Many of our communities are disconnected, and in some cases, we don't even know our neighbors' names. This would never have happened a generation ago, and it forces us to reevaluate and develop a new way of living.

Not only do we need a new strategy for dealing with the challenges of day-to-day living, but we also need an entirely new money strategy. Money isn't the same today in many respects as it was yesterday. We put a different meaning on it. We've come to depend on it even more than previous generations, and the investment a person makes in self-development directly impacts his or her ability to be successful with money.

Get Real!
Reinvent yourself

As I've helped people over the years pursue their goals financially and otherwise, I've discovered that being able to adapt to the 21st century challenges us to *reinvent* ourselves in many ways: how we raise our families, what we do with our time, how we take care of our physical health, and how we think and operate with regard to money. Today is a new opportunity, and we aren't limited by what we once thought to be true.

You no longer have to see yourself as someone who just gets by, simply because that's the way it's always been, perhaps for generations. You no longer have to view yourself as the person who earns only enough to pay the bills, because that's just the way it's always been. You do not have to be the person who never has anything left at the end of the month, just because you, your parents, your grandparents, or your great-grandparents never had anything left before. *Developing your ability to think in new terms with new strategies and in bigger numbers is all part of reinventing yourself.* I'm not suggesting that a new money strategy is all there is to self-development, but it makes a huge difference, considering that most people in America wake up every Monday morning and go about making money in the same way again, and again, and again—*the same old way, using the same old money strategy.*

The question is, "How do I reinvent myself in order to have a more abundant financial life?" It begins by telling yourself the truth. I want you to get really good at calling things what they are. Quit cheating yourself by believing what may not be true. It's tough when you begin asking yourself hard questions:

- ■ Do I have beliefs or habits that are stealing my dreams?

- ■ Do I let my emotions control my behaviors in negative ways, giving me results I really don't want?

- ■ Do I blame others for my situation only to keep myself stuck longer?

- ■ Do I overreact to situations and become destructive to others and/or myself?

Best-selling author Phillip "Dr. Phil" McGraw says in his book *Life Strategies,* "The only thing worse than having a child on drugs, a serious disease, or a philandering spouse is having the problem but not recognizing it, or, worse yet, knowing it but *pretending* it isn't true."[1] Let's quit pretending that our financial situation isn't directly related to our thinking.

Get Real!
You have total control over what you choose to think

Being honest about what you think you do know and what you don't know about money, as well as being honest about what you really deep inside believe about money, will give you a huge advantage to getting the actual results you want.

---

1. Phillip C. McGraw, PhD, *Life Strategies* (Hyperion, 1999).

As I've trained people in the subjects of money, business, investing, and self-development, I've found that the vast majority of people in America have a real need for real-life strategy in these areas. Financial knowledge is clearly not one of America's strengths. It's a weakness, a major weakness. People know more about the weather, sports, TV shows, and where to fish, golf, and dine than they do about money, how it works, how to get it, how to keep it, and how to make it work for them. Yet most people spend most of their lives *trading time for dollars*, not really knowing the principles, concepts, and strategies regarding the stuff they're trading life for!

In America, we need a whole lot more than *more* information. We need the *right* education, clear step-by-step direction, and the *inspiration* that leads to *transformation*. We need to change the old thinking, the old systems, the old beliefs, the old ways that just don't work anymore in this day and age. Either we choose to adapt, or we get eaten alive!

By using *Get Real! Strategies*, you'll have a new game plan, including step-by-step actions; begin the process; prime the pump; build momentum; and get results. It takes keeping an eye on the target. It's about focusing your mind and looking forward, creating something that isn't already there. *Get Real! Money* is not a onetime thing you do or a single book you read. It's changing the way you play the game by embracing your own personal reinvention.

Get Real!

Embrace change

Think about it for just a minute. You probably wouldn't be reading this if you didn't want something different in your life, especially something financial. *Change is positive*, even though we've trained ourselves not to think so. It's time to reinvent the way you view what's going on around you and to genuinely embrace change. You can, *and you must*. If you don't embrace change as a way of life, your future will be even more turbulent. Most of us grew up in times of enormous change. The problem was that we weren't prepared for it. Nobody showed us how to prepare or how to effectively deal with it. Today we must be prepared to deal with the changes we experience every day and will continue to experience as the pace of change accelerates—social changes, economic changes, everything. We aren't stopping the tide of change, no matter how much we like or don't like it, and we must have the ability to deal with it in an enjoyable, productive, and positive way.

If you want new results, it all begins by changing something. I don't suggest you leave behind your moral values or personal code of ethics. Those remain in place unless they need changing. You may change your viewpoint as you grow. However, values shouldn't change just because our society and environment changes. We've got to know *how to successfully adapt* to the world we live in without losing hold of what we truly value. Now I'll begin to show you the new game plan for financial security and how to adapt to this changed world of money.

CHAPTER 3

The Get Real! Game Plan for 21st Century Success

IMAGINE LIVING YOUR LIFE on old financial ideas destined for failure, yet hoping somehow, some way, some day, that old idea will work just because you hope hard enough. Can you afford to trust your future to old, outdated ideas that are leaving most Americans living paycheck to paycheck?

Here's the real American dream today: *not having to work for money*. Imagine that—living in America, enjoying the great freedoms and luxuries, and not having to work. That's what most people call "retirement." Well, now's the time to *get real* with the facts and perhaps reinvent your definition of retirement. By the way, if you're younger than some of us, you, too, will figure it out real soon: You won't want to *have* to work for money forever.

Get Real!
We're living a lot longer

Here are a few reasons you will need to reinvent your idea of retirement. Today, we're living longer—a lot longer. The average life expectancy for men and women in the United States is about eighty years. Many more of us are living well into our nineties and even past 100. The demographics of our society have changed dramatically since our parents' day.

In the 1930s, when Social Security was enacted, the average life expectancy for men was sixty-two. Social Security was instituted to be supplemental income specifically for widows and those well into their senior years. It wasn't designed as a retirement fund for every person who ever worked and could still work. Today, the majority of politicians don't like to talk about the realities of the financial condition of the Social Security system; it doesn't get them elected. According to *USA Today* (January 20, 2003):

> **"Last week, the General Accounting Office, the auditing arm of Congress, issued a chilling report. Without badly needed reform, Social Security is rapidly headed for financial ruin. . . . Acting today to make Social Security solvent in the long term would require a 15 percent hike in payroll taxes."**

I don't know anyone who wants another 15 percent taken out of his or her paycheck before payday. If we continue much longer, we'll have a lot of disappointed baby boomers when their time to retire arrives. The over-85 population is expected to rise by 54 percent to 6.8 million by 2020. These people will need a place to live, and most likely government assistance. The question is, who is going to pay for it?

Get Real!
Don't get trapped in your senior years being dependent on government assistance

Currently, the government covers about 60 percent of the cost for elderly assistance, mostly through Medicaid. It also requires you to become almost dead broke before qualifying for some of these benefits. So what happens when a huge population of old baby boomers need government-assisted living? Things will have to change. If we wait for the system to change to our benefit, we're going to be in big trouble. Our children and grandchildren aren't about to elect people who raise taxes on their take-home pay by 20 to 40 percent. At some point, everybody must get his or her head out of the sand. The *ostrich strategy* doesn't work too well.

People who attend my *Get Real! Money Seminars* range in age from eighteen to ninety with the majority in the thirties to sixties. However, I am beginning to see an increasing number of attendees, who are well into their seventies and eighties. These people are seeking help for their financial future. The vast majority of people in America are still buying into the illusion that they will be financially set once they reach retirement age. That's just not living in reality.

Get Real!
Don't get caught in the illusion

In the last century, if you wanted financial safety and security, it was a decent strategy to find a large, stable company to work for that provided retirement benefits, a few weeks of vacation, health coverage, and consistent work. That was a great idea fifty to seventy-five years ago, but that financial model has disappeared in America and doesn't work anymore. Don't get caught in the trap of thinking everything is going to magically work out. You may be the nicest, the most generous, the least selfish person on the planet, but that doesn't exclude you from the reality that the game has changed—and it's not going to come back in your lifetime.

Get Real!
Reinvent your idea of retirement

Today, America needs a new definition of *retirement*, and you must develop a new strategy to achieve it. Most people think of retirement as a time when they'll have enough money coming in to not have to work and plan on this happening somewhere between ages of sixty and seventy.

Imagine for a moment a new kind of retirement. Let's call it *financial independence*. Become independent of the need to work for money by learning how to make money work for you. Imagine working because you want to work, not because you have to. Imagine making it your goal to get there as fast as possible. Here's my definition of financial independence:

> "I have the free time and financial security to do the things I want to do—when I want to do them."

Who said you must be sixty to seventy years old to get there? That's part of the old plan that most people follow. Some of them will be waking up one day, taking their heads out of the sand, and hearing the news that Social Security checks won't be delivered until age seventy to seventy-five, if ever. Medicare benefits are being cut, and the government doesn't have the money to house you in your golden years.

Look at history and you'll find that only over the last 100 years did we actually *invent* the idea of retirement. Before then, people didn't retire. They became the respected elders of the family. They were highly esteemed, well respected, and sought after for wisdom and advice. They didn't plan to simply stop working forever. The idea of not working is relatively new in our culture. Of course, people didn't live as long either. Things changed, and people *invented* the idea of retiring. And now things have changed again. We're now living in a world where people are not only living longer but, in many cases, are considered unemployable by age fifty!

In America, we're living an average of thirty years longer than we did 100 years ago, and we're desperately trying to survive on a 100-year-old financial strategy that's long outdated and broken. We get halfway done with life, and we're considered unemployable because we expect too much from employers who can't possibly deliver. Most people at age fifty aren't willing to make the sacrifices a twenty-two-year-old would make for a career commitment. Fifty-year-olds want paid time off, retirement benefits, health insurance, employment security, and on top of that, they want a seasoned employee's income.

Employers, on the other hand, are looking at the price of the stock. They realize they can hire a person right out of school who doesn't have all the demands a seasoned employee does, is willing to work longer hours, is newly educated in the knowledge economy—and besides, they can hire that less experienced person for two-thirds the salary!

You see, as a society we bought into the idea of the *job* during the Industrial Revolution, which eventually resulted in unionized labor with negotiated benefits from employers in return for employees' work commitment. In the long run, that commitment has turned many people in America into slaves of the system that's now eating them alive.

Get Real!
Develop a plan for financial independence

Most people are expecting to have retirement money magically coming from one or a combination of three places. Let's get real and look at each:

1. Company retirement plan

2. Social Security

3. Personal savings

Company Retirement Plan

In 1974, the Employee Retirement Income Security Act (ERISA) was made law, changing the way corporations deal with the retirement of employees. Before ERISA, companies had what is known as a defined *benefit* plan versus what we have today, a defined *contribution* plan. A defined benefit traded a certain amount of years for a predetermined retirement income that would continue for the rest of your life. A defined *contribution* is much different.

When ERISA was passed more than a quarter of a century ago, it was thought to be a benefit to employees. However, it actually became more of a benefit for the *employer*. The expense of retirement transferred from the employer to the employee. Now we have defined contribution retirement plans such as the 401k, in which the *employee contributes* to a fund and the *employer matches* a percentage of the money contributed by the employee. The problem: *Most people in America don't contribute much*. Therefore, the employer has little or nothing to *match*. Statistics show that people aren't contributing much to their plans. Also, consider the fact that most employers provide retirement benefits only after an employee is *vested*, which in most cases means full-time employment three to five years. Only after a person is vested can he or she begin taking advantage of the defined contribution plan. Today, the American worker doesn't expect to be employed at the same place long enough to create a significant retirement saving through a defined contribution plan. The whole idea of ERISA, which sounded great at the time, has backfired on the employee, as the next generation of retirees are finding out.

Social Security

Retirement plan number two is Social Security. If you're currently enjoying Social Security benefits, enjoy. Take whatever you can get. I project that most of us won't see much for our money. Plan on a Social Security check being the whipped cream on the sundae, if there is any at all. Just make sure you know where the banana and ice cream are coming from.

Personal Savings

And finally, retirement plan number three: personal savings. It's impossible in this world to work hard enough and to *save* your way to retirement. Statistically, we have reached an all-time low. According to the Organization for Economic Co-operation and Development as reported in *The Wall Street Journal* in June 2004, average household savings have gone from 0 percent in 1991 to a -1.2 percent in 2002—which is not good.

Get Real!
You must *invest* your way to retirement

Saving will take a major sacrifice and discipline, but you must also have a structured and accurately executed investment strategy, starting as soon as possible. You can't put it off another year, because every year you put it off now will cost you multiple years in the future.

I remember talking to my first financial advisor when I was only nineteen. He strongly suggested that I be sure to open an IRA that year. I sat there thinking to myself, "What in the world does the Irish Republican Army have to do with me?" I knew enough to know that I didn't know what he was talking about, but was bright enough to ask, "What's an IRA?" He told me I needed to start planning for retirement as early as possible and that I should set up an Individual Retirement Account and that it would be a great tax savings. I looked at him sideways and thought to myself, "Retirement—he's got to be kidding. I'm only nineteen years old, and I'm practically broke."

He encouraged me to invest $1,000 in a *mutual fund* (by the way, I had no idea what a mutual fund was either). He said, "Some day you'll look back, and you'll be very happy you did." He told me that if I continued to keep this money invested for the next forty-five years and if it grew at 15 percent per year, I would have $500,000 in my retirement account. I took his advice. That one small investment was the beginning of what has grown into my investment understanding and my portfolio of investments. That single account has grown and grown, as well as given me confidence to begin many other accounts using many other types of investments.

Given these three options, what will be your *plan?* How will you become financially independent? You may be in the majority of Americans who have neither retirement money nor plans in place. Before I met many of my students, they didn't either. You may not have one penny saved or a company retirement plan in place. You probably realize that Social Security is not going to do much for you. You may be like countless others who made considerable sacrifices to put some money away and tried your best to make it grow, only to be disappointed with the results. I want you to know you aren't alone. Most people in their forties, fifties, and sixties have almost no money and no real plan. *But I also want you to have hope that there are answers, there are solutions, and I will show them to you.* Let's first define what your financial future can look like.

Get Real!
Join the New Normal™

As mentioned earlier, Americans are finding whole new ways of living differently. Today it's common for people to have three and four careers in a lifetime. Maybe they hold down a job as well as start a small business on the side, maybe they leave a job and go full time into business, or perhaps they work for a company as a consultant and buy investment real estate on the side.

It has become *normal* to change careers midstream or develop additional income streams on the side as well as never actually retiring. Today we are redefining a new way of living that involves being flexible enough to change and reinvent ourselves to meet our desires for different lifestyles. I call this the *New Normal*. The New Normal is a cyclical lifestyle following career and lifestyle choices as opposed to the *linear lifestyle* of our parents in which there was one life plan that took them from birth to retirement.

Get Real!
Never stop working

Now, how about you—what's your plan and what's going to be your definition for retirement? Do you want to retire or become financially independent and able to do things you want to do when you want to do them—and have the money to do it?

Imagine not having to work—just working because you want to, not because you have to. Some of my favorite people are the folks who never stop. They work *because they find purpose, enjoyment, and fulfillment from work.* Did you know we were designed for work? We are not put on Earth to simply pay our dues, then sit back and not keep busy. Work is healthy. Work keeps us moving forward; it keeps us alive. Staying active and financially productive part-time is good for the body, mind, and soul as long as you don't have to. You'll never hear that from the Social Security Administration or your boss.

I had a wonderful experience a few years ago when I needed a document notarized. I hired a notary who came by the house in order to save me time. She said she could be by at 6:15. I said to her, "That's about the time we eat dinner. Can you make it earlier?"

"I meant 6:15 a.m," she said.

"Now, that's too early," I said.

The notary explained that was the only time she could do it, so I agreed. Well, the next morning she was in the driveway at 6:05 waiting for her appointment. I was amazed to meet this vibrant eighty-four-year-old woman who was operating her part-time notary business before she went to work part-time!

Evelyn the notary was dolled up, upbeat, and enthusiastic. She did her job with precision, cheerfulness, and excellence. What a privilege it was to meet and be inspired that morning. I didn't ask, but I assume she was this energetic busy bee, involved and working like this because she wanted to, not because she had to. I've decided I will never completely stop working unless I'm unable to.

You need to *choose* a new way of living. It puts another whole spin on how you view the meaning of work and how much you enjoy it. It's the new normal of today's cyclical lifestyle. By the way, I'm not saying you should never kick back. I'm suggesting that instead of completely retiring and never working again, make work something you do because you want to. Then, without killing yourself, choose to work from time to time doing something you enjoy, with people you enjoy, staying active and continuing to reach for more. In fact, plan on it now—you may not have another choice.

Get Real!
Define what financial independence means to you

To become financially independent, you must define what that means to *you*. Put some real numbers to it, and then back up those numbers with a plan. Keep in mind that, when doing financial forecasting, there will always be variables that make it an imperfect calculation. The best thing to do is calculate your projections conservatively and be reasonable with your expectation so you won't be disappointed. Let's look at the four primary variables (I call them money factors) that everybody needs to deal with when doing a financial forecast.

Get Real!

Take into consideration the four primary factors of any rock solid financial plan

Money Factor #1: Expected Life Span

It's amazing to realize that we're living thirty years longer than people did 100 years ago. Medical science has adapted and found how to *prevent* diseases that were killing us 100 years ago—we never actually cured them. For example, 100 years ago the primary causes of death were flu, pneumonia, and tuberculosis. We never discovered how to cure these conditions, but we've learned how to prevent them. Today, the leading causes of death in America are heart disease, stroke, and cancer. In fact, we've discovered a lot about preventing all of these, and life expectancy continues to rise. Is it possible you may live to be 100 plus? What happens if you buy into the sixty-five-year game plan like many people do and you end up living to be 99 or 103 like my grandmothers?

Money Factor #2: Cost of Living and the Time Value of Money

Today, on average, we live eighteen years in retirement. How will the cost of living affect the lifestyle of an individual who retired at age sixty-five and plans on living on a *fixed* income when he or she ends up living well into their nineties? On average over the last 100 years, the cost of living has increased at just about 3 percent per year. This means the buying power of money is constantly decreasing by 3 percent annually. Ask anyone living on a fixed income. It isn't easy. After a few years it becomes evident that it isn't fun! Besides, they've worked their entire lives and now they *finally have time* to have some fun. Suppose they have grandchildren and want to spend time with them spoiling them a bit. It all costs money! Imagine retiring on half to two-thirds of what you were living on when you were working. That's quite a cut in your lifestyle—and you've just retired!

You must take into consideration the *time value of money*. Over time, the value of money decreases because its buying power decreases. The same $50,000-a-year income today will have only $20,600 of buying power thirty years from now adjusted for inflation.

Money Factor #3: Investment Rate of Return

An investor will earn either a "fixed" rate of return or a "variable" rate of return. Whenever you opt for a fixed return, you are taking less risk and are rewarded with a smaller return. The opposite is true for a variable rate of return. When you take a variable rate of return, you are willing to flow with the ups and downs, the changes in the markets you invest in. You may at one point receive a higher rate of return than the fixed investor, and at another time you end up with less. You'll find more on investing in chapter 10.

Money Factor #4: Unexpected Events

Life is filled with the unexpected. Most of my students over the years have been blindsided at least once. These events can be financially devastating. They do happen, and they happen to most people at some point in their lives.

Health problems, relationship setbacks, child problems, job loss, and physical accidents are all uncontrollable events in life. No matter how well we plan, we can't control everything. All you can control is how you deal with them. Either way, you've got to move forward with your financial plan, hoping for the best, yet being realistic. *Stuff happens* that will change all the best of intentions overnight. I suggest you plan for the best, yet temper it with these things in mind. Suppose your only form of income comes from physical labor. What happens if you physically can't do that work any more? It's time to adjust your expectations and make another plan. As a professional speaker, I realize that the income I derive from speaking could end instantly because of a situation I don't control. So I've developed other sources of income to create a diversified income base, which creates a safety hedge in case that happens.

You will need a *financial independence game plan* to reach the goal. It doesn't just happen all by itself. I'll be giving you definite investment details in chapter 10. For now, you must get in touch with your real desires concerning your financial future.

Financial independence comes only to those who diligently pursue it with self-discipline. Ask yourself these questions, which will help you get in touch with what you want, and if you want it badly enough.

- How will I feel if I *have to keep working* well into my seventies or eighties even though I don't want to?

- How will I feel about myself if I become dependent on government assistance for food and housing?

- How will I feel about myself if I never get out of debt?

- How will I feel if I have nothing left to pass to my heirs?

- How will I feel not being able to enjoy the simple pleasures in life, such as dining out or golfing once in awhile?

- How will I feel not having extra money to give my grandchildren for presents?

I could go on and on. I know what you may be saying: "Oh, not me! This will never happen to me." Maybe you need to visit a few government-subsidized assisted living facilities and ask these people their story. I have. You'll find smart, educated, hard-working people who spent years providing for their families. People that were just like you. I'm afraid America will be filled with old baby boomers who are flat broke sooner than they think. Yes, you do need a new game plan for the 21st century.

Get Real!

If you're not working on a financial *independence* game plan—you're working on a financial *dependence* game plan

The question really isn't *whether* you need a plan. I know you understand that. The question is more a matter of *when* you plan to achieve your goal. I suggest you choose a year that you are working toward. Forget choosing an age; just go with the year. I've worked with young people who are well on their way as long as they stay the course. And I've worked with thousands of older people who are starting from scratch again. Some of our greatest American legends have amazing stories to tell. Henry Ford was forty-two and unable to buy a Christmas tree for his family. J.C. Penney was nearly bankrupt in his sixties yet went on to phenomenal wealth. Colonel Harland Sanders of Kentucky Fried Chicken fame was tight on cash in his late sixties while getting KFC off the ground.

Yes, I do understand that starting older is challenging—but the best comes out when we are most in need. I've also found that with age comes wisdom. Practical insights from the lessons of life are extremely valuable in the real world of money-making. I have had the privilege of being involved with many intelligent older Americans who are improving their financial lives in their senior years. I'm amazed by them and what they have accomplished.

Get Real!

Include in your plan a provision for major expenditures along the way

Part of your financial game plan will need to include money for the major expenses along the way toward financial independence. Raising children, caring for elderly parents, and improving current living conditions are just a few of the costly items along the way that need to be planned for. All these things cost money. Decide now, rather than later, that you will need more money. Be sure to take action on the things that create more money, so you will be able to reach your goals. Do not procrastinate any longer!

Get Real!

Develop a mental picture and plan for living a long, healthy, and active life

As you age, plan what you want the future to look like. Are you looking forward to healthy living, being in good physical condition, and enjoying your life? What is the picture you see and carry with you everywhere you go? Your plan contains a mental picture of your future. Don't wait until you are there. Get a clear picture now, so your mind will direct your steps and create opportunities for the fulfillment of your dreams.

As you put together your game plan to get real money, you must include each of *The Five Master Money Strategies* discussed in the next chapter.

The Four Money Factors of a Rock Solid Financial Plan

Money Factor #1: Expected life span

Money Factor #2: Cost of living and the time value of money

Money Factor #3: Investment rate of return

Money Factor #4: Unexpected events

CHAPTER 4

The Five Master Money Strategies

THE FIVE MASTER MONEY STRATEGIES are the foundation to a successful financial future in the 21st century. For many people, the *Five Master Money Strategies* will remain secrets—forever. They remain secrets, until a person *wants* them and uses them. But once you know them, and once you use them in your own life, their power is yours—forever.

Imagine yourself deciding to build a building. You'll need three parts:

1. A game plan

2. A foundation to build on

3. Materials that have proven to work

This is exactly how you will build your financial fortress. It begins with the *Get Real! Game Plan for 21st Century Success.* The foundation will be the *Five Master Money Strategies*, and the building materials will be the *Five Proven Money Principles.*

GetRealMoney.com
The Five Master Money Strategies™

#1 Personal Growth Strategy
Money Risk-Free

#2 Tax Defense Strategy
Money Protection

#3 Investing Strategy
Money for Life

#4 Free Enterprise Strategy
Money Security

#5 Real Estate Strategy
Money Safety

© 2005 New Discovery Media Corporation

If you continue to operate your financial life using strategies and ideas of the past, you'll continue to get predictable results, which is the law of cause and effect. The question is, are you happy and excited about the results you've been getting? If so, wonderful—keep using what works. However, most people want *new results*. Learning and using the *Five Master Money Strategies* will create new results.

Financial author, the late Charles J. Givens, once said, "There are three things we are never taught in life—how to have a good marriage, how to raise good kids, and how to manage money."[1] *Specialized self-education* goes a long way in each of these areas. These aren't the kinds of things we're taught in high school.

The other approach to life works like this: Hit your head against the wall for ten, twenty, or thirty years, and wake up one day realizing you really don't like the results you have. Maybe a little specialized information in the form of self-education would have made a difference. If fact, if you had learned

---

1. Charles J. Givens, *Wealth Without Risk* (Simon & Schuster, 1991).

the information presented in this book years ago and acted on it, where would you be today? *The school of hard knocks is cheap to get into, but expensive, time-consuming, and hard to get out. It teaches us the lessons after the experience!*

Get Real!
Tap the resources of those who already know the secrets

One of the fastest ways to accomplish almost anything you want is to tap into the knowledge and experience of people who have already been there. They know exactly what *not* to do. They've already made the mistakes and know which road leads to where you want to go. They know the shortcuts. They're called experts. We at the *American Financial Education Network* conduct special educational teleconferences on business, real estate, and investing to name a few, and you are welcome to attend. Visit www.GetRealMoney.com\resources for details. These informative phone trainings are an easy way to develop additional money-making knowledge by simply listening in.

It's time to get excited about becoming educated for the challenges of the 21st century. It's time to put away the old model of education. It doesn't pay like it used to. In the 20th century, if you had a college degree, you were marketable. Today, you can have a master's degree or a Ph.D. and find it difficult to obtain work you enjoy that's also financially rewarding. A college education may not be enough. And when it isn't, you need to know where to find education that delivers results. I have trained thousands of individuals with college degrees who were seeking to learn the information for running a business, buying wholesale real estate, investing properly, and generating new forms of cash flow. This type of information just isn't available through most *traditional* channels of education. That's one of the reasons I formed the *American Financial Education Network*. I wanted to provide a way for people to easily access the specialized education, resources, and tools they need for financial, business, and personal success.

As a student, you may have been like me. I was one of those kids who just didn't click well with a traditional classroom setting. I was the one who talked a lot and instigated others (which means I caused my teachers lots of trouble), and those skills certainly didn't equate to high IQ or test scores. I've since learned that I am highly intelligent, although I didn't feel that way for many years. I've become self-educated by studying at several colleges and by reading or reviewing thousands of books and articles as they related to my personal growth. I've attended many advanced education seminars and listened to hundreds of tapes and CDs on a variety of topics. I've consulted with and been mentored by some of the most successful people in their fields. Most of all, I've learned by applying what I studied. There is no better teacher than experience. And I keep learning. I continue to read, study, attend seminars, hire professionals, listen to audio recordings, and apply what I'm learning.

Get Real!

Specialized self-education ignites action, which creates success, which builds confidence— which raises self-esteem

Education coupled with action creates success. Success builds confidence. Confidence leads to a higher level of self-esteem. You'll need confidence in the area of finance in order to have more money. You'll become a highly confident personal money manager as you continue to learn and then apply what you learn here.

Specialized Self-Education ➡
Take Action ➡
Create Success ➡
Build Confidence ➡
Mastery and High Self-Esteem

Get Real!
Join the Cyclical Lifestyle Generation

According to Ken Dychtwald, author of the book *Age Wave*, "We are witnessing the dissolution of the traditional linear life plan. In its place, a much more flexible arrangement, known as the *cyclical life plan*, is emerging."[2] The cyclical life plan is a significant change and has been taking shape in our culture over the last thirty years. In the past, people expected to finish their education by approximately age 21 and then proceed into the world of work.

Work or career would last approximately thirty-five to forty-five years before coming to a time of no work called retirement. This is the pattern that most of our parents experienced. It was simple, it was predetermined, and everyone knew what was expected. This is considered a "linear" approach versus the "cyclical" approach of today.

Today, it has become the norm to redefine "what I want to do with my life" in terms of work and career. This one factor creates a need to begin a new "cycle" of learning and developing new skills, which require an investment of time and money. Today, people are more and more interested in maintaining healthy relationships, for example. They decide that selling out to a career that demands most of their attention isn't what they want in life. They've decided career advancement is not worth the compromise of putting family life on the back burner. In many cases, this attitude results in not getting the promotion, which in turn means less money. This impacts the linear approach and creates a new cycle.

I consistently see students in my seminars who are in their sixties, seventies, and eighties. These people amaze me with the dreams they are pursuing at this point in life. It's wonderful to be a part of what they are accomplishing. But these cyclical go-getters are just the tip of the iceberg of what's coming.

2. Ken Dychtwald, *Age Wave* (Jeremy Tarcher, Inc., 1989).

I project that I will be doing exclusive programs just for people in these age groups. Why? Because I already see it happening. People are getting older. People are figuring it out. Life is a process of constant growth, and the people who stay active are the ones who enjoy a more fulfilling life. Also, many of these people are starving for financial help in their later years. *Financial self-education* will play a major part in everyone's future.

Look at the participants at one of my recent *Get Real! Money Seminars* on how to start and build a small business. There was an energetic and irresistible woman named Ruth, who at the age of seventy-three had just released her first music CD. She sought help on how to promote her work. And then there was John, who at age sixty-three had just barely made it through cancer treatments. The process had drained him financially as well as physically. He had previously owned more than twenty pieces of rental property and was doing quite well before the incident. He was restarting his money-making machine and needed strategic planning support.

I've worked with many people who at a "ripe young age" are just now reinventing themselves. I tell my younger participants (anyone under sixty) that these folks in their seventies, eighties, and even nineties are ahead of their time. In the near future, it will become the norm for the majority of people in their later years to be developing new ventures and new streams of income, starting businesses, creating new forms of cash flow, and learning how to invest intelligently—all because they need to *reinvent their financial lives.*

I can't tell you how appreciative I am of these people and what they have done for me. They have provided me with a clear example and vision of possibilities in my own life as I reach their age. They are the true leaders of the new cyclical lifestyle.

Our generation wants more and expects more from life than previous generations, creating the need for a new way to deal with these ambitions. People are also forced to develop new skills because of the changes in the economy. Economic changes have created massive changes in the job market. A person must have other options in the works today. The job that is here today may literally be history tomorrow, because our economy has permanently changed. All of these factors are pushing people toward a cyclical approach to life. This cyclical approach must include retooling for the present day as well as the future.

Get Real!
Make pain your ally

One of the greatest challenges for many members of my educational organization is: "How do I get myself to do what I know I need to do in order to be successful?" This is a master key to your success. It's one thing to know what to do, and it's another to know how to get yourself to do it. We are creatures who shun pain. You want to use the process of moving away from pain to lead you in the direction of less pain—the place you want to go.

Life is like the corner of a room. Two walls eventually meet in a ninety-degree corner. When we get ourselves into corners, we have three choices:

- **Option 1:** We can walk further into the corner *not even aware* that our options are closing.

- **Option 2:** We can turn around, put our backs to the wall, get real, and acknowledge that the options are becoming fewer and fewer.

- **Option 3:** Once turned around, we can drive a stake into the ground and secure ourselves to it, making sure nothing we can control will force us any further into the corner—then we can work on getting out.

By driving the stake deep into the ground, we begin moving away from the pain. Get in touch with the pain of what will happen if you don't take action. Realizing how painful it will be not to take action and seeing what results will occur and how painful those results will be can cause us to choose differently. By applying discipline and action now, even though it is painful, it will be less painful than not taking action. We move away from the place of pain to a place of less pain.

This is part of what we already are doing quite naturally. Acknowledge that your life is going to be financially excruciating if you don't take action on the strategies outlined in this book. If you leave your financial life to chance, you will be making a huge mistake and will no doubt regret it some day.

The next step is to engage—get real, get mad, and get going! Nothing replaces the power of taking action. Action begets a physiological response and conditions us for forward momentum. It's true, you can't steer a parked car. You've got to do whatever it takes to get unfrozen and get moving. You've got to read books, take seminars, surround yourself with forward-moving people, do whatever it takes to get unstuck—today. My hope for you is that this book will be an explosion in your life, an impetus, to do just that.

Commit yourself to something today that will keep you on a path of momentum. Yes, finish this book as fast as you can, then reread it, make notes, write down action plans. Write down your goals. Daydream, get free, and get out of the rut.

Get Real!
Distinguish between what you can control and what you will choose not to try to control

In a sense, this chapter is about taking control. There are so many things in this life we cannot control, but most of them we can. Wisdom is in knowing the difference and acting positively with momentum.

The one variable is *you*. You've been given the privilege and the responsibility to control your thoughts, actions, and attitude. What you read, how you behave, who you associate with, what you watch on television are all factors *you* control. If you're in the habit of winging it day to day, your environment is controlling *you*—I guarantee it.

Have you ever been on a seafood diet? You *see* food, so you eat it? You walk past the TV, click it on, and vegetate for an hour or two or three. Hey, we're all guilty, but now it's time to be aware and take control of the temptations in our environment. Honestly ask yourself: "Where are these influences really taking me?"

Commit yourself to becoming responsible for the environment in which you live, realizing you have the power to choose and control your environment. Become self-reliant and do not depend on others to do it for you. Business philosopher and colleague, Jim Rohn, says it well: "Are you waiting for someone to motivate you? Well, what happens if they don't show up?"

Don't forget that your environment also includes your state of mind. You are entirely responsible for your attitude. Not the weather, not your spouse, not circumstances, and not the daily news. You can make excuses all day long, but ultimately, you're responsible for what you think and feel.

Commit yourself to a future that is yours to design. Decide to become a self-managed individual who does whatever you can to increase your success rate and enjoy living in the moment. Developing self-mastery is difficult and challenging, but it's worth the effort. I can guarantee no one is going to do it for you. You're either committed to the process of reinventing yourself through self-education, or the winds of chance will be glad to do it for you.

One of my favorite early teachers was radio personality Earl Nightingale. He said, "Success is the progressive realization of worthy ideals." I personally needed to redefine success for my life. I used to think that some day I would *be* a success. It was always some day—not today. You may be able to relate to this. Then I realized I was never able to get there. Even though I had achieved, by many people's standards, a high level of success, I still didn't *feel* successful. I was always hurrying on to the next success and never enjoying the moment. I have now redefined what success is to me. It's not a destination. It truly is the progressive realization of worthy ideals. *Success is the journey.*

Get Real!
Define success

Are you laboring under the same misunderstanding? Do you have a clear definition for success? Success is in the *being*. *Success is in the moment, not the future.* Just by the fact that you are reading this material, in my view, makes you a successful individual. You are putting effort and time into building your dreams. Do you want success in some area of your life? Really want it? Then define what success is to you, perhaps even use this definition for yourself. It's here, it's now, and you are already a success. Success is the progressive realization of worthy goals.

Get Real!
Develop successful habits and skills

To be successful in the present, you will need to begin developing successful *habits* and *skills*. This is not an option or just a good idea. Successful people do things differently from the rest of us. It's not because they are better; they just want different results. For you to have the things you want—be it financial success, relational success, health success—you'll have to get real about what you are willing to do to get results. Ask yourself, "Am I committed to developing skills, learning information, and exposing myself to new ideas that will help create a new reality?" Decide what results are important to you. Later on I will have you write down some of these. I will show what skills and information you must learn and develop in order to accomplish the results you're after.

Trying to get the results without making the necessary shifts in actions and thinking will only frustrate you and result in failure. Frustration and failure do have their place for the person who is growing. However, you don't want to fail for lack of effort, or by being naïve.

Get Real!
Determine to take action

Another factor in determining your success is in knowing *when* you want the results in your life. Considering that this book is about money strategy, how long do you wait before debts are paid off, until your cars are free and clear, until you have more money at the end of the month versus living paycheck to paycheck? How much longer are you going to wait?

It amazes me how people really believe they can continue putting off driving their stake into the ground and just drift further and further into the corner with no options left, rather than making the decision to get busy making things happen. In America, the vast majority of us have our basic needs met, and so we choose to put off until tomorrow what we could do today. Are you ready to stop putting off developing a financially secure future? Do you want to work day after day, grinding out a job that you hate? Do you want to have the freedom to determine when and how much you work?

You know you can't keep putting these issues off. Get real, decide what you want, and get on with it. One small step per day compounds itself. Three months, six months, one year down the road, you won't believe the difference you've made by taking action now.

Get Real!
Give yourself permission

It's time to give yourself permission to be successful. I realize that perhaps your mother or father may have told you otherwise. Perhaps it's your spouse or your neighbor who thinks it's not okay to be successful. Well, that may be okay for them—but you need to determine what is right for you.

The truth is, you are designed for success. However you define success, it's yours for the taking. As long as you don't hurt other people in the process, you'll do fine. I realize that some of you reading this don't need that lecture. However, from my experience working with people—most do! I know I did.

Decide what you want ➡ Choose to do it ➡ Just do it!

Get Real!
Live to your full potential

Have you ever noticed that no living creature other than human beings lives to less than its full potential? Have you ever heard of a tree growing only half as much as it could have? Have you ever heard of a squirrel gathering only part of what it needs to survive a long winter? Isn't it amazing how we are gifted with the ability to choose, yet many choose to go only a third or half the way? Choose to go as far as you can.

Living is a wonderful process of learning, exploring, and trying. I have heard that basketball great Michael Jordan once said, "I have missed more than 9,000 shots in my career. I have lost almost 300 games. On 26 occasions, I have been entrusted to take the game-winning shot and I missed. I have failed over and over again in my life. And that's precisely why I succeed." Perhaps you've tried to better yourself in the past and failed. Maybe you tried to launch a business or buy real estate and failed; or not completed something you started. In the real world, that's exactly how to succeed.

Join the club. We've all done it. I've personally failed many times. In fact, I've come to realize that unless I'm failing from time to time, I'm not in the hunt and keeping forward momentum. Failure is a necessary part of the personal growth process.

In the next chapter, I'll share the secret of how to turn failure into success.

CHAPTER 5

Master Money
Strategy #1

Get Real! Money Risk-Free: Personal Growth Strategy

MOST PEOPLE ARE TAKING HUGE FINANCIAL RISKS and don't even know it. Getting real money isn't about taking risks—it's about using proven money strategies and *avoiding the risks that do not lead to money.* In this chapter, I will show you how to eliminate unnecessary risks by being committed to learning the right strategies that will lead to real money. The first of the *Five Master Money Strategies* is *The Personal Growth Strategy*™. Personal growth begins by knowing how to use failure as a teacher.

By embracing our past failures, we can learn from them and, in doing so, not repeat them. Years ago I learned to keep an *experience equity journal.* That's a written list of what you've learned from the mistakes you've made. What lessons and conclusions can be drawn from the experience in order to develop real wisdom? Then, just as important as writing in the journal is reading it from time to time in order to keep on track and be sure you're not repeating the same mistakes. There's one risk you can avoid—making the same mistakes over and over.

Get Real!

Correct and adjust often; make new decisions with new information

As we follow a game plan of action, it's exactly like flying an airplane from Los Angeles to New York. The plane takes off with a definite flight plan and destination. Along the way, the plane is off track 99 percent of the time. The pilots and computers must make hundreds of *corrections and adjustments* along the way to ensure that the plane lands at the right place and within a few minutes of the flight plan schedule. Neither the pilot nor the plane's computers knew exactly what disturbances would be encountered. They are prepared to *correct and adjust when necessary*. Your experience equity journal can act as a guidebook of lessons so you become a better and more prepared pilot for the next flight. Successful people are prepared to make *new decisions* when they have new information. Don't get stuck thinking your one idea is the only piece of information you'll ever need for your journey—that's a risk. Imagine taking off from Los Angeles to New York and being one degree off-course, and meanwhile, you never make any corrections. You could end up at the North Pole!

Personal Growth Strategy

The *Personal Growth Strategy* embraces several specific ideas from balance and momentum to using the subconscious and eliminating excuses. Let's look at some concrete ways to reinvent yourself and master the *Personal Growth Strategy*.

Get Real!

Balance the past, present, and future

Let's look at balance first. How do we balance and put in perspective the past, present, and future? Yes, we are in the present. However, we are in the present with all our past experiences and all our future expectations.

Actually valuing all three and fully living in the moment with passion, anticipation, and a mountain of wisdom gathered from the past develops our sense of balance in order to enjoy the process we are going through. We can't just ignore, forget, or pray away the past. Yes, we can learn how not to let it have a negative hold on us. However, the past is part of our present experience and our gateway to our future.

Getting real with ourselves and being strong enough to face and reconcile painful experiences from the past are the best ways we know for dismantling the power these experiences have over us in the present. In some positive way, we've got to deal with a painful past in order for us to reach our full potential in the present and the future. Not learning from past failures is a risk too many people take.

Get Real!

You are either moving forward or slipping back—but there is no such thing as standing still

Taking action in the present is essential for our self-development and financial success. There is something magical that happens when we actually *do* rather than merely *think* about doing. Taking action is the door to a better financial future. It may be as simple as making a few notes in a journal or reviewing a chapter in a book. It may be making a new contact or getting your first business card. Action begets more action. The more action you take, the more momentum you create. It's the snowball effect. It starts with one flake, turns into a snowball, then rolls into an avalanche. Applying the 7 *Minute*

Secret consistently will compound into success. Remaining stagnant is a major risk.

Inaction kills momentum. Fight against inaction and learn to just—*do it now*! I have gone to the extent of posting "TAKE ACTION!" stickers on my desk as well as on the windows and doors in my office. Action always creates positive momentum. Yes, you will stub your toe from time to time. You might even feel as if you are moving too fast. But it's better to be moving too fast and hitting a few bumps than slipping back. One of my early mentors taught me the momentum principle. She said, *"Don't kid yourself, Jim, you are either moving forward or slipping back—but there is no such thing as standing still."* If you want to avoid financial risk, if you want financial safety, don't kid yourself—you're either moving forward or you're slipping back, but there is no such thing as standing still. Kidding yourself is the real risk!

Get Real!
Put in place the Law of Use

Another *reinvention principle* is called the Law of Use. The idea is to never despise small beginnings, to be thankful with what we have, and to take action with the resources we have. In business and real estate investing, we call this *bootstrapping*. I've launched multiple business ventures and bought real estate, beginning with practically nothing. I simply took the raw material I had in front of me and made lemonade out of lemons.

The most successful people you'll ever meet are those who started with nothing and made it happen despite the odds. These people didn't get "lucky." For example, a family friend went through a separation and a divorce several years ago. She and her two teenage children were left with no money, no support, and a trouble-making ex-husband. She proceeded to pull herself out of the mess; she got a job, started going to school on the side, and received her degree. Today she has climbed the ranks to a senior position working in a healthy environment in an occupation she loves. She has put her children through prestigious universities, just bought her first house, and on top of that, found love again and married a wonderful and successful man. That's the Law of Use—in action.

When you take what you have to get started, you put into play the Law of Use and the Law of Momentum at the same time. When you are faithful with little, more will come your way. For those who are engaged in action and have created momentum, making the most of what they have at that moment always generates more opportunities. For the person who is inactive and waiting for someone to come along and do it for him or her, there is always the question of why good things seem to happen only to other people. And the person will be wondering that for the rest of his or her life.

Get Real!
Develop the power of perseverance

The next key to reinventing yourself is developing perseverance. You must learn to be tenacious. It takes courage to fly. The good news is that you can develop your level of command in almost any area when you put your mind to it. It takes time. Realize that these are necessary ingredients for success. People who have successful families and successful relationships and are financially successful have developed all they have in a trial by fire; they have persevered through many challenges.

Get Real!
Prepare to pay the price

Learning to *pay the price* is essential for success. In fact, success doesn't come any other way. There isn't any BIG EASY, because if there was, you would probably have discovered it by now. It's about preparing and then paying the price. Many people are under the illusion that there must be an easy way out. They are living in a dream world, and when they wake up, they will be disappointed.

Whether we realize it or not, we all pay the price. It's a matter of either pay the price now or pay it later. The price of perseverance, courage, discipline, and tenacity is much less costly and painful than the pain of regret later. Don't get stuck thinking there's an easy way up.

Get Real!
Get excited about discipline

The next key to reinventing your money and your life is discipline. Discipline plays a major role in the results we achieve for ourselves. I mean discipline in mind, body, and spirit. I have to work hard disciplining myself, and I have great admiration for those who have excellent control and mastery over themselves. For me, discipline comes down to two simple factors—choice and focus.

There is power in choice; we decide what we apply ourselves to. There is power in focus; we can develop focus as we exercise the necessary discipline. Embrace and enjoy discipline. Ask any athlete and he or she will tell you it's painful to feel the burn of pushing past physical limits, but it's in the burn that new muscle is developed. When muscles are being pushed to their limits, they are able to grow. Find a way to push yourself into highly disciplined environments. Become acquainted with disciplined people. You'll find them all around you—at the gym, in the health food store, at seminars, on the jogging trail. I can almost guarantee you won't find many at the all-you-can-eat buffet, McDonald's, the slot machine, or playing the lottery.

Get Real!
Discipline your mind

Developing discipline is all in your mind. Learn to become aware of your thinking by making notes as to what you are thinking and the way you are processing your thoughts. Become self-aware. A great way to do this is by keeping a private journal. Writing out your thoughts will help your mind develop clarity. Ask yourself questions, remain objective, and be honest about your answers.

Our thinking creates our reality. If what we're putting into our minds is not the reality we desire, we had better make adjustments. We must surround ourselves with pictures, ideas, books, videos, CDs, environments, and people who we feel are healthy and in line with what we want to create. By doing so, we provide a platform to stimulate our conscious and subconscious minds in order to give back the reality we want.

If you want joyful, positive thoughts, be around joyful and positive-thinking people. Listen to relaxing and/or motivating music or informational CDs versus songs that aren't in line with your values. Eat at places where healthy people eat. Seek out television shows that inspire and motivate you in the direction you want to go versus shows that simply entertain. Putting ourselves in environments that are healthy and directed toward what we want is vital to positive personal growth. Feed the mind, body, and spirit healthy high-quality food rather than the typical day-to-day junk.

Get Real!
Ask yourself the "right" questions

Develop the ability to ask questions in a positive manner as opposed to negative. The mind is constantly processing thoughts, and is working consciously and subconsciously at the same time. We need to take charge of the way we permit our thoughts to operate. First, realize that you do talk to yourself. In fact, you *self-talk* all day long. You're doing it right now! One of the best ways you can direct your thinking is by asking yourself the *right* questions. In the example below, try turning the question from a negative one into a positive one.

Why am I always having this problem?
turn into
How can I solve this problem?

Why can't I seem to get out of debt?
turn into
How can I bring more money into my life?

Your mind will answer any question you ask. Decide which questions you really want answered and what results you want your subconscious to bring out. You will find that the more successful you become, the more you have the skill and ability to think in ways that provide you with the results you want.

Get Real!

The subconscious mind doesn't distinguish between truth and lies

As your subconscious mind processes information, it does so without bias as to whether or not the information is true or false. It just accepts it as fact. The subconscious is not like your conscious mind, which logically processes your thoughts. That's why it's important to monitor what you feed your mind. Information finds its way into the subconscious and will produce powerful results, good or bad.

By writing down your thoughts, you'll develop an awareness of what you are really thinking. Unobserved thinking is like music just rambling though the mind. Have you ever noticed how when you hear a song on the radio early in the morning, you can hardly get it out of your head all day? The subconscious mind is most receptive just as you are waking up and just as you are going to sleep. Use these prime times as opportunities for feeding your mind quality food. Reading an inspirational book or listening to positive music during these times will make a powerful impact.

An excellent way to solve personal problems is by asking the right questions during these moments and then patiently waiting over time as your mind searches for solutions and finds avenues to answers you may have missed. Be prepared to write down the answers as they come to you over the coming days. Inventor Thomas Edison was known to sit in a chair letting his hands hang at his side over metal plates on the floor. In each hand was a steel ball. As he would drift off to sleep, the balls would drop from his hands and the noise would wake him up. He would then quickly take notes of his ideas, at that very moment, in search of solutions for his inventions.

Get Real!
Use powerful words that create impact when speaking to yourself

The next step is to identify words that have power. The words we use when speaking to ourselves influence our response. Marketers know it, psychologists know it, and you need to know it. To best self-manage your own life, you need to choose your words carefully.

One word I have chosen to eliminate from my life is the word *can't*. I've replaced it with *choose* or *choice*. I am empowered by the word "choice" and bound by the expression "can't." I can—I just choose not to. By doing this, it puts me in control and helps eliminate any sense of my being powerless in a situation.

Look for words or phrases your mother told you not to say, such as: I hate, you're stupid, you idiot, what a fool, etc. These are self-limiting phrases. Discover and use words that empower, such as: I can; I choose; I will; I am; I know; I will find it; I can do that; I need this; I believe; I'm intelligent, motivated, creative, genius; I like myself.

Get Real!
No Excuses Strategy™

Another key to personal growth is to monitor the excuse-making that most of us do. Once you realize what excuses you are making, you can begin to turn them around and use them as a weapon. When you hear yourself say phrases such as I'm too small, too big, too thin, too fat; I don't have enough money; I have too much money, no time, and so on, admit it—these are excuses plain and simple. Here's America's all-time favorite: *I don't feel like it.* Ha, ha—let's face it, there are millions of things we don't *feel* like doing in life that we must do. Once you have trained yourself to hear the excuse, then you are able to attack the situation by doing the exact action you are procrastinating about when making the excuse in the first place.

Get Real!
Attack the excuse immediately

Attack the excuse immediately. Don't let it get away from you. It is so empowering to look the excuse in the face, then conquer it before it conquers you.

My grandmother lived to be more than 103 years old. She was a terrific woman. When I phoned her, I would ask, "Hi, Grandma, how are you?" The reply was always the same for years and years. "Why complain?" she would say. This woman lived an incredible life, living by the creed that nothing good comes by complaining, so even though I may have things to complain about, I'm going to *choose* not to! Wow, what a strategy. It's the half-full glass of water versus the half-empty.

Get Real!
The truth sets you free

What happens if you don't tell yourself the truth about reality? The lie will continue to eat away at you. Whatever it takes to get out of denial is what you need to do. Truth is worth knowing, seeing, and following. Anything less than the truth is a lie. Truth does set us free. Denial about a situation does not. This happens many times in people's finances. The fact is that they are drowning themselves financially, and they keep on hoping and wishing it wasn't true. So they end up sinking deeper and deeper into debt.

Do it differently than everybody else. We don't have to do it like them. The truth is the best place to begin. It's the place we turn our ship around. It's the place we stop slipping backwards and begin moving forward.

Get Real!
Focus your mind on the results you want— not your fear

The next key to powerful personal growth is to overcome and break through your fears. Focus your mind on what you want— not what you fear. Fear can and will consume you. It will paralyze and can kill you. Don't let fear stop you from getting and having the things you want in life.

I have learned that the best way to conquer fear is by acknowledging it, facing it, and disarming it by walking right into it and doing that which I fear. Yes, some fear is warranted, but most is not. Most of the time fear is not based on reality. It's based on lack of information and is designed to defeat us. Don't let it happen.

Get Real!
Create enough desire for what you want in order to face and overcome your fear

Once you know what you are afraid of, you can develop a strategy to deal with it. Ask yourself, where did that fear come from? What fact is it based on? Why do I think I'm afraid? Then ask yourself: Is this the truth? Who can help me? Once you've come to grips in your thinking regarding fear, combat it with focused desire. Get a crystal-clear picture of exactly what you want and why you want it. As you remain focused, the focus itself will create power and energy to overcome the fear you are dealing with. Overcome fear by focusing your concentration on what you want—not what you are afraid of. If you could become laser-focused on exactly what you want, do you think you'd be more effective at getting it? Of course, you would.

Gaining experience equity, making corrections and adjustments, learning from mistakes, building momentum, taking action with what you've got, disciplining yourself, asking the right questions, making no excuses, and focusing on what you want (not what you don't want) is the pathway to *Get Real! Money.* By doing so, you have eliminated many unnecessary risks. Remember, there is no such thing as standing still; you are either moving forward or slipping back. The real risk is in thinking that we can stand still. Now that you are moving forward, let me show you the ultimate strategy for creating financial safety.

CHAPTER 6

Cash Flow Safety Zone

WE ALL HAVE DEFINED BELIEFS about money. These core beliefs about money in turn become our operating principles. Whether you realize it or not, you are already following certain principles, and these principles impact your financial life. Some of these beliefs create financial safety, and some create unnecessary financial risks. In this chapter, I will show you the best strategies for creating a *financial safety zone.*

Get Real!

Get real and be honest about how you *feel* about money

I'll ask you a few simple questions, and I want you to give them some thought. I want you to begin by picturing where you come from in terms of your financial beliefs and where they're pointing you.

One of the toughest struggles for most Americans, even though they don't realize it, is *poverty thinking* or *poverty mentality*, as it is also called. Some see money in life as a constant *lack versus abundance*. It's the feeling of being stuck and not in control because of external forces. This belief puts a person at-risk and outside the *safety zone*.

Have you ever heard yourself make any of the following statements?

- I can't afford it.

- It costs too much.

- I guess I'm not supposed to have money. It must not be meant to be.

- Why am I always broke?

- People with money hurt other people.

- They must have done somebody wrong.

- We're not from that side of the tracks/neighborhood.

- We're not like them.

- I'm just not good with money.

- Money is too complicated for me.

- I'm not good with those things.

- If only I had money, I could make money.

- This is just the way it is.

- It will always be this way.

- We'll never have the money.

- Somebody "owes" me.

- If only I were taller, shorter, smarter, or didn't have this or that person in my life, I'd have money.

These statements are symptoms of a deep-rooted belief that a person is lacking something. They are self-limiting scripts that produce limiting results and a lack of money in life.

Get Real!
Self-limiting beliefs produce limited results

The beliefs that we hold produce exactly what we tell ourselves to produce. If you want different results, you must look seriously at what your current internal programming is telling your subconscious. This isn't just theory; this is fact! Today, we clearly understand the correlation between our thoughts and our results. We must ensure that our thoughts are in line with the results we want. If they aren't, we become frustrated. Our first goal is to define what we are telling ourselves, and then define new scripts to get different results. If you want to discover financial safety, make sure you are aware of your scripting as it relates to money.

One of the easiest ways to get a picture of our money beliefs is by examining what our parents modeled for us. If your parents ignored financing matters, just got by, and paid the bills, guess what? These are the life scripts they handed to you. Is that what you want—to just get by—or do you want more? I thought so. It's simply cause and effect. If you find yourself in debt, perhaps afraid of investing, perhaps not believing it is possible to have more money than you absolutely need every month, that's what you'll get. Perhaps you came from a home where only one parent handled all money matters and the related responsibilities were all left up to just that one person. Have you ever heard this one: "Get a good education and you'll get a good job?" How has that one worked for you? It's time to identify scripts that produce the kind of results you *do* want.

Get Real!
Identify what you know you don't want in order to define scripts of what you do want

For most people, including myself, it's easier to identify and put into words what you know you don't want than to explain exactly what you do want. Once you define what it is you don't want, you can easily turn that statement into a positive script of what you do want. Take a minute and write down a few results you know you don't want, such as the following:

- I don't want to be broke.
- I don't want to be stressed about money.
- I don't want to have arguments about money.
- I don't want credit card debt.
- I don't want to have a car payment.
- I don't want a mortgage on my house.
- I don't want to be living from month to month.
- I don't want to be broke when I get old.
- I don't want... I don't want...

Then you reverse them to:

- I want to have more money than I spend every single month.
- I want to feel free of stress.
- I want every credit card paid in full every single month.
- I want no car payment.
- I want my house free and clear of any mortgages.
- I want to have plenty of money to enjoy myself when I get old.
- I want... I want...

It's important that you get real about your beliefs concerning people, finances, and the idea of owning and running a business. If you hold any negative beliefs about wealthy people, or the idea of owning a business, your internal belief system won't permit you to become wealthy or own a business. Have you ever heard yourself say something like: "They have money because they take advantage of people" or "People with money are snobs"?

I have found just the opposite to be true. The majority of people with money and/or in business are the most generous, hard-working, kind, influential, courteous, smart, and interesting people on earth.

Get Real!

Get real about your beliefs about people, finances, and business

To get the results you want, you must, first, discover what you believe about:

1. Money—abundance versus lack

2. People with money—good or bad

3. Business in general—good or bad

Then you can make the corrections and adjustments to your personal self-limiting scripts.

Yes, there are people who have money and own businesses who are cheats, are unhappy, and hurt others—just as there are people who don't have money or don't run a business who are crooks, are unhappy, and hurt others. You must decide which you're going to be, and then become it. If you have never been around people of means, you'll discover these people are typically some of the most generous, interesting, kind, hard-working, caring, and conscientious people you will ever meet. Generally speaking, these people are principled, sincere, courageous, and have integrity. I didn't always think this myself. I've had to work on self-limiting scripts in more then one area of my life, too.

Get Real!
Money equals choice

Bottom line: money equals choice. The more money you have, the more choices you have. Do I eat fast-food or do I eat at a nice restaurant? Do I live in the neighborhood with the schools I want or in a neighborhood with schools that I don't like? Do I drive a financed car, or a car I own free and clear? Money gives freedom and the power to choose.

It's the difference between being a slave to money or choosing to be free of money problems. I'm not saying that having more money settles all of life's problems, but it sure makes having the problems a lot less difficult. In fact, many of the typical problems that people must deal with are directly related to money. You may have the desire to help the less fortunate. The best way to help the poor is to not be one of them—simple choice. You may not want to work every day of your life; that is a choice and you must be the one to make it. If you want to have money for investing, it's a choice and you must make it. There's dignity in having the ability to choose. There's freedom in having a choice. It's more fun having choices.

Get Real!
Write down some of the choices you'd like to have if you had more money

What are some of the choices you'd make if you had more money? Would you get out of debt, spend more time with your loved ones, help the less fortunate? It's time to write these choices down. How would you recreate? What would you do, where would you go, who would you be with?

You might aspire to help others in your community by having more money. Who would you choose to help? Are you interested in helping disadvantaged children in your community, or people in need in other parts of the world? It's liberating when you begin to feel the awesome power of choice. Let yourself think freely of the potential. Imagine money funneling through you to help others.

- What would you do?

- Where would you go?

- Who would you be with?

- What would you do to recreate and have fun?

- Who would you give to? (charities, nonprofits, churches, individuals in need)

Many students come to my *GetReal! Money Seminars* wanting to develop additional income to help family, friends, churches, and charities. I always make it a point to help them get their personal financial houses in order first. By doing so, the time and resources to reach out to others will become available. Trying to give time and money you don't have doesn't work. I'm in favor of helping others, but getting out of debt and reaching the point where you're putting away hundreds or even thousands of dollars every month is the best way to help others. Then you will have the clarity of mind, the money, and the time to help those in need.

Get Real!

Get inspired by other prosperous and generous people

Get inspired to be a giver. Get inspired to be generous. Get inspired to become prosperous well beyond your month-to-month needs. See yourself as a funnel for money flowing through you to benefit others. One of the best ways to become inspired is to be around people who are generous toward others. Through their example, you'll develop not only a desire, but an understanding of how it can become possible for you as well. Learn from these people. Ask them their stories and how they got in a position to be able to give.

Develop a *new financial vision* for yourself by learning from others. Focus on what you want, and you will begin not only to develop new scripts, but also to believe it is possible for you, too. Then you'll be able to do what it takes to accomplish your goals and at the same time enter into the *cash flow safety zone*.

So many people are just short-sighted when it comes to life's possibilities. Human potential expert and colleague Mark Victor Hansen says, "There is no such thing as a shortage of supply. There is abundance everywhere, and it is meant for you to have. Your receiving what you want will not take away from anyone else. And don't worry about the *how* when it comes to receiving abundance. The only thing you must deal with is the *what*."[1]

Becoming a possibility thinker is about coming to terms with your personal human potential. The people who aim high, have great vision, and apply themselves are the people who accomplish great things.

A personal business manager of a well-known country music artist once told me it was his client's goal to have $1 million in the bank. That would be her ultimate financial achievement. She would feel wonderful having accomplished her goal. For her having a $1 million in the bank would mean financial safety and security. She is clearly a possibility thinker who knew what she wanted and was disciplined about getting it.

The Cash Flow Safety Zone™

The good old days of having one source of income are now history. It's a huge financial risk to depend on only one form of income today. Our economy has shifted from a labor-based manufacturing economy to a knowledge-based service economy. A single and steady job has become more and more

1. Mark Victor Hansen, *Rich Results*, Week 5 (Hansen & Associates, Inc., 2003).

elusive for most. I tease my older friends who worked for close to forty years with one company. I call them the last great dinosaurs of the 20th century. The idea of a permanent, stable job is extinct. I've had thousands of students who have been either let go, laid off, displaced, or downsized. The world has changed, and it is a must to develop multiple forms of cash flow in order to create financial security. I'm not referring to having your spouse or partner work, too, or getting another job. Yes, that is another cash flow, but wouldn't you rather have only one of you working full time and perhaps the other building a business or developing an income stream of passive investment income? The *Cash Flow Safety Zone Strategy* is simple: Diversify your income—by creating multiple streams of income—to create a cash flow safety zone.

Get Real!
Create a safety zone by diversifying your income sources

Imagine having money coming to your mailbox week after week—from various sources other than another job. Everybody can afford the investment of time to develop other income streams on the side. I realize that we live in a busy and frazzled world, but most people still expect to have time to sit back, take it easy every now and then, and watch a little TV. I understand, I do, too. But think back to our ancestors for a moment. They didn't have the luxury of taking coffee breaks, watching TV, or going bowling. Many got up before dawn to do their chores. They worked in the hot sun or the factory all day with few breaks. Then they would take a quick dinner break and work some more. They slept only to wake up and start all over again, six or seven days a week, month after month, year after year. Many did this well into their later years just because that's the way things were. They didn't have the luxuries we have today. Most of us today don't even know how to fry chicken, milk a cow, or plant a seed. We're far removed from days gone by—so far, in fact, that I believe America has gotten soft when it comes to our expectations for comfort.

Have you ever noticed that current first-generation Americans are hard-working and many are extremely prosperous? Many own the corner stores, the gas stations, the restaurants, and the real estate. Many feel that their lives are easy, considering where and what they came from.

Don't short-sell yourself into thinking you don't have enough time or opportunity. That's classic poverty thinking. It destroys your future and puts you at-risk. That's focusing on what you perceive to be what you *lack*. Instead, focus on the *possibilities* and the potential. See your life and your future as full of abundance rather than full of obstacles. Everyone can develop additional forms of cash flow if they want, even while working a day job.

Having several forms of cash flow creates stability and security. Study the chart on the opposite page for a few minutes. One cash flow is dipping, while the other is rising. That's the nature of cash flow, winter, spring, summer, and fall. Sometimes it's up, and sometimes it's down. By creating multiple streams of income and diversifying your income, you create a *cash flow safety zone*. Notice how the safety zone widens as the number of cash flows increase. This safety zone will never come from holding down a job. One form of cash flow is not safe. This safety zone also creates a secure feeling, because you know you're not relying on just one stream of income.

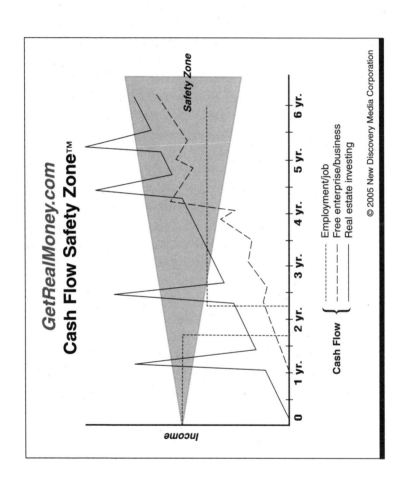

CHAPTER 7

The Five Proven Money Principles

THERE ARE *Five Proven Money Principles*™, which are the basis for acquiring, accumulating, and protecting your money, that work for everyone, every time. Once you learn them and apply them, you'll begin to see results almost immediately.

People who follow a long-term thinking strategy accumulate wealth. They work hard, they start with what they have, they have no hidden advantage, they are committed to a long-term plan utilizing proven principles, and they take action! It's not about winning a lottery, or getting an inheritance, or the get-lucky syndrome—not at all. People who fall into money generally have never learned *how* to be wealthy. Once they get money, considering they didn't know how to get it, they lose it all or spend it in a matter of years. J. Paul Getty's great book is called *How to* Be *Rich*, not *How to* Get *Rich*. We *become* rich in mind, body, and spirit in the *process* of acquiring wealth. Then and only then are we truly rich. Becoming rich isn't something that just "happens" to a person because he or she has money. It's a process based on applying the *Five Proven Money Principles.*

Proven Money Principle #1: Think Long Term

This is how you win with money. Thinking in one-, three-, five-, or ten-year increments is essential for your financial success. If you are like me, you grew up in a short-term-thinking generation. We want to have what we want—now. We want it convenient and easy; we don't want to wait or work hard for it. That's the reason I taught you the *7 Minute Secret.* I know our generation can manage it. One or two generations ago they had few choices and didn't think in these terms. They knew they had to pay their dues. These were the World War II, Korean War, and Vietnam War generations. Many lived through the Great Depression.

They grew up understanding *delayed gratification.* It was a way of life. Our generations come with different expectations, which have created a belief system that runs counter to building real long-term wealth. We've grown up in a short-term-thinking world that says, "Watch a TV show, buy an electric belt to put on your stomach, and wake up with a six-pack of muscles, right?" Well, in reality, we know that's not the way it works. But that is the way many *think* it works. Many believe the TV, radio, and magazine ads that tell us we can have everything now. We obey what they feed our minds. If it looks good, feels good, sounds good, our generation pretty much believes it to be true. Decide to develop a long-term mind-set in everything, especially money. It's proven to work.

Proven Money Principle #2: Pay Yourself First

Whenever money comes your way, discipline yourself to *pay yourself first, before anybody else.* Pay yourself 10 percent of all the money that goes through your hands first, *before anyone else gets a part of it.* This discipline will develop a new meaning for money in your life. Most people spend every nickel that goes through their hands almost immediately. They pay the mortgage company, the credit card company, the car finance company, the electric company, or the government. We weren't given a destiny in life to work, work, and work just so others can take our money and our lives every month. They want us to think that way, but we know better. Unfortunately, most people are well trained to do just that. Work, get taxed, get paid, then pay everyone else first. Month after month after month. By paying yourself first—allocating 10 percent to your *money plan*—you are taking control. I want you to make the usual payments for credit cards, cars, and house mortgage *after* having taken the 10 percent off the top. This 10 percent will be used for debt reduction, building an emergency fund, and free enterprise. Eventually, this will be used exclusively for long-term investing.

See yourself as so important that you must be the one to pay first. If you don't, you never will. This is a financial success habit that develops as you consistently remind yourself to do it. If you don't, you'll pay everybody else and have nothing left for you. You must reverse that thinking, develop discipline, and start taking care of putting yourself first when it comes to money. This is all part of developing your *money muscles.* It's the belief that by helping yourself you will be better able to help others.

By paying yourself first, you will have money for long-term investments. A 10 percent long-term investment savings plan plants the seeds of long-term thinking. This means putting 10 percent away, intending never to spend it. This discipline also enables you to develop an emergency fund should your financial situation change. I want you to have an emergency fund of at least six month's living expenses. This fund is used only for an emergency, and should be in liquid savings such as a money market mutual fund. You don't want to wait until your credit cards or cars are paid off before you start your emergency fund. Begin funding it right away, even as you are paying off outstanding debts.

You'll find you can still get by, even on 10 percent less. In reality, 10 percent won't break you, and you will be able to make the adjustments necessary to make it happen. Once you have paid off your debts and set up an emergency fund, continue to pay yourself first, putting 10 percent into long-term investment accounts.

Now you've developed a 10 percent habit and laid the foundation for taking another 10 percent of all the income going through your hands and planting the money in an enterprise that potentially pays you year after year. This 10 percent needs to be activated with discipline, effort, and commitment. That's why having a business or a service you provide is essential. Not only are you developing another income stream, but you are also actively involved in the process of *growing your money*.

You must move away from dependence on your employer or the government. Start developing a new perspective of money stewardship. Developing a plan that gives you the results you want. It's time to get a solid grasp on how to make money work for you rather than you working for it. *You become the master of money and move away from being its slave.* That's what investing and free enterprise are all about. Making money grow by compounding and personal effort is exciting. We invest our time, our ideas, and our sweat equity to cause the 10 percent seed to grow. It all begins by making sure 10 percent comes right off the top after you have paid yourself first. We'll further discuss investing and enterprise in a later section.

Proven Money Principle #3: Use the 10-10-10 Rule

Your eventual goal will be to pay yourself 30 percent first before anyone else gets paid.

1. 10 percent for charitable giving
2. 10 percent for long-term investing
3. 10 percent for free enterprise (making more money)

To arrive at this point may take you several years. You must go through several other growth steps. You decide when and which charitable endeavors—religious affiliations, charities, or people/families—you want to help. As a matter of habit and financial discipline, I believe 10 percent giving to charities, the less fortunate, and religious affiliations should be done before long-term investing and free enterprise. Please visit www.GetRealMoney.com\resources for credible organizations that are outstanding at helping the less fortunate. A percentage of the profits generated from this book are used for helping disadvantaged children throughout the world.

Paying yourself first and following the *10-10-10 Rule* are *financial success habits*, and the sooner you act to start them, the sooner you will experience the benefits. Personal enterprise, such as a small business or the purchase and resale of wholesale real estate, will become a source of money to supplement your emergency fund, long-term investment, and charitable giving. The more consistent and disciplined you become in handling your money this way, the greater results you'll have.

Here are the steps to take to get the *10-10-10 Rule* completely in place:

- **Step 1: Emergency Fund.** Set up a money market mutual fund account at a local bank and start funding it. Even if you are starting with only $10, do it now, not later! You should begin funding this at the same time as you are taking steps 2 and 3.

- **Step 2: Debt Elimination.** I'll show you later how to simplify this process in another section of this book.

- **Step 3: Investment Fund.** Set up a mutual fund account and start funding it—again, even if with only $10. Find suggestions on how this can be done at www.GetRealMoney.com\resources.

- **Step 4: Enterprise Fund.** Set up a *separate* money market fund at a local bank to be used exclusively for enterprise activities, which we'll discuss later.

Your emergency fund, investment fund, and enterprise fund *must be three separate accounts*. Don't make the mistake of combining them. That will defeat the purpose. If you have to use separate envelopes to keep them divided, then do it.

Proven Money Principle #4: Live Below Your Means

The secret is to not spend it all—simple. Live on less than you make. This is *the* financial problem in America—most people spend it all, plus more! It's time to live below your earnings. There has to be a point where you stop spending everything you make. Millionaires become millionaires by not having spent it all and by following these exact principles I'm showing you here. The majority of millionaires drive used cars, live in homes smaller than they can afford, and don't have big-screen TVs. It's the complete opposite of what you might expect. Real wealth is what you accumulate—not what you spend. Other people spend tomorrow's cash today, the exact opposite of what it takes to become financially independent.

Thomas Stanley and William Danko, authors of *The Millionaire Next Door*, point out, "They [millionaires] create an *artificial environment of scarcity* for themselves and the members of their household."[1]

You, too, must have an artificial environment of scarcity for the money that goes through your hands. Without it, you'll

---

1. Thomas J. Stanley, PhD, and William D. Danko, PhD, *The Millionaire Next Door* (Pocket Books, 1996).

spend it all. In the world of money, you're either planning to win or, by default, you're going to lose. There are just too many temptations, predators, and mistakes you can make. Believing you will succeed financially without a plan is a plan to financially fail.

Too many people want a piece of your money. You must be decisive, proactive, and disciplined. You can afford to put off other things like watching TV, shopping at the mall, or bowling. But when it comes to money, don't make the mistake of putting off working your money plan. It's time to commit to developing new money habits, new ways of viewing money, new approaches to controlling your money, and a real-life proven approach to handling the money in your life.

Proven Money Principle #5: Master the Time Value of Money

The last of the *Five Proven Money Principles* is to understand the "time value of money." *As time passes, money is worth less and less.* A dollar today has significantly less buying power than a dollar did ten years ago, and the impact can either financially make you or break you. (Take a moment to study the time value of money charts on the following pages.)

You may be old enough to remember the 1965–1966 Ford Mustang. You could buy a Ford Mustang for only $2,000. Imagine that, a beautiful new Mustang for $2,000! Today that car is worth close to $25,000. It's basically the same car; it just costs a whole lot more. In today's dollars, $25,000 has about as much buying power as $2,000 did forty years ago. Do you remember the old Volkswagen Beetle? In the early seventies, it cost $2,200! Today a VW Beetle sells for more than $20,000. *The purchasing power of the dollar erodes with time.* As the cost of living increases, the purchasing power of money decreases.

I'll never forget that first house I bought. I paid $28,500 for it in 1979. An older neighbor from across the street came over to introduce himself; he laughed when he heard I had

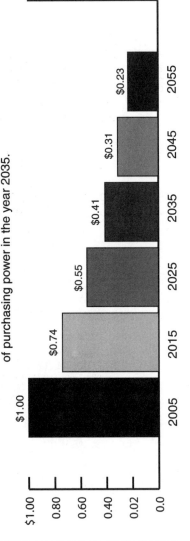

GetRealMoney.com
Time Value of Money #1

The Shrinking Dollar

$1 of purchasing power in the year 2005 will only be equal to 41 cents of purchasing power in the year 2035.

2005	$1.00
2015	$0.74
2025	$0.55
2035	$0.41
2045	$0.31
2055	$0.23

Scale: $1.00, 0.80, 0.60, 0.40, 0.02, 0.0

*Calculations are based on the assumption that the cost of goods and services (CPI Index) will average a 3% annual increase, and the currency valuation of the U.S. dollar will also maintain a historical value over time.

© 2005 New Discovery Media Corporation

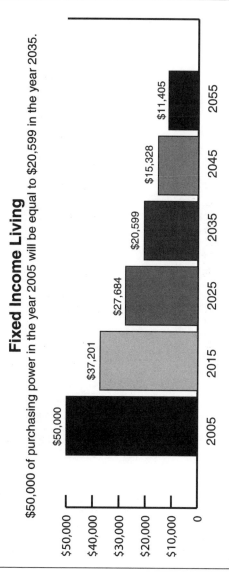

Get Real! MONEY

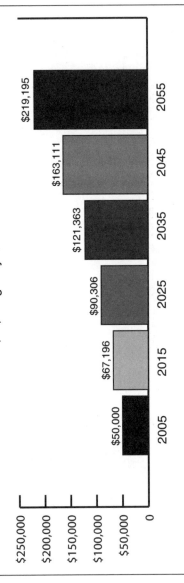

GetRealMoney.com
Time Value of Money #3

Maintaining Purchasing Power

In 2035, you will need $121,363 in income to have the same purchasing power that $50,000 gave you in 2005.

2005	$50,000
2015	$67,196
2025	$90,306
2035	$121,363
2045	$163,111
2055	$219,195

*Calculations are based on the assumption that the cost of goods and services (CPI Index) will average a 3% annual increase, and the currency valuation of the U.S. dollar will also maintain a historical value over time.

© 2005 New Discovery Media Corporation

bought the house for so much. I felt hurt and didn't under-stand why he found it so funny. He went back to his house and found a picture of the house I had bought, but the picture of the house was taken fifty years earlier. The house had been offered to him at that time for $1,500! When I purchased the house, it wasn't a better house; it was just fifty years older. Money was worth much less then. Interestingly enough, I sold that same house for $148,000 some years later. My older friend wasn't laughing then.

Get Real!

Work from your head, not just your heart (emotions)

Take care of yourself first, develop a healthy self-interest, and apply the *Five Proven Money Principles*. Soon you'll wake up and be amazed at how healthy you feel and how proud you are that you have made the investment of time and energy to de-velop your personal financial confidence.

Let's now finalize one more major step before you can implement your *Get Real! Game Plan for 21st Century Success*.

The Five Proven Money Principles

Proven Money Principle #1:
Think long term.

Proven Money Principle #2:
Pay yourself first.

Proven Money Principle #3:
Use the 10-10-10 Rule.

Proven Money Principle #4:
Live below your means.

Proven Money Principle #5:
Master the time value of money.

CHAPTER 8

Eliminate Debt—
Fast and Forever

COMING TO TERMS WITH DEBT ISN'T EASY.
There's nothing comfortable, fun, or enjoyable
about it. If you're in debt, join the well-attended
and well-funded fan club of millions of American
families who, on average, have more than $6,000 in
credit card debt. Knowing this doesn't fix your problem but at least you know you aren't alone.

Get Real!
**Get real truthful with yourself about your
financial situation**

You might not find yourself in debt at this time, but
I suggest you *not skip any part* of this book. Many
smart people who are now in debt weren't at one
time.

To begin clearing debt and turning your financial situation around, you've got to *get real!* We can
only change things we acknowledge. Once you

acknowledge your debt situation, you can make the decision to get out of debt. Yes, you are in debt, it hurts, it's not a picnic, and you better get committed to turning it around, because your situation will not improve by itself. However, the good news is: you got yourself into the mess, and you *can* get yourself out of it.

I want to be perfectly clear about this—*there is hope*. Hope begins when you realize and admit you're in trouble and need help. And it's okay to need help. It's time to start really evaluating *why* you've ended up where you are. It's time to stop blaming somebody else, even if it is their fault. You're the one with the debt, and you're the one who must get yourself out. Millions have pulled themselves out of serious debt once they realized and admitted what happened. There is hope, you're not alone, and as you start using the strategies in this chapter, slowly but surely good things will start to happen for you, too. Thousands of Americans every year use these proven strategies to pull themselves out of the quicksand of debt, and it's entirely possible for you to get through to the other side as well. The last thing you want to lose is hope. I'll show you now how you can begin the process of helping yourself and also how to get help from others. Take a deep breath and prepare for the long haul.

Get Real!

Put the brakes on all spending until you evaluate your situation

The first step is to stop the financial bleeding. You must make serious adjustments to your financial thinking and spending habits. You must not keep doing the same things and expecting different results. Put the brakes on all spending until you completely and objectively evaluate your situation with a competent third party, if necessary. It may help to put your financial details on the table with a person who knows what to do in your situation. I'm not talking about your husband or wife or friend or neighbor. I'm talking about a debt-reduction/counseling specialist. Visit www.GetRealMoney.com for a detailed action plan called *The Debt-Free Living Action Plan* under Credit Repair.

Getting the support of a third party will give you hope to see your situation from another point of view—the other side. This person can help you to see options you can't see from where you are. Collect all your financial data to properly and thoroughly evaluate it. You will need a list of all past due accounts, credit card account numbers, phone numbers, utility bills, mortgage account numbers, checking accounts, bank accounts, etc. By putting it all together in one place, you organize yourself and your finances so you can get a handle on them.

Get Real!
Adjust your expectations

To turn this around, you must *adjust your expectations*. Again, it's about delayed gratification. Debt is created by spending more than you make. People fall into the credit trap of borrow, borrow, borrow. Borrow for a nicer car, a bigger house, nicer and newer furniture, new clothes, and new toys. You've got to decide that it's not financially healthy to buy on credit. It's not good to buy *stuff* you can't pay for *right away*. If you are not able to make the payment that month, don't buy it.

I want you to get angry about materialism and the overexcited consumer mentality in your life. We're living in an unrealistic society, filled with companies that exist to make a profit—not to keep you out of debt. In America you've got to be on guard. You can bet that credit card companies and home equity lending institutions know the precise statistics regarding what percentage of customers won't be able to make the payments. They have it figured out to a T—and they bank on it.

Get Real!

Learn from your financial mistakes—don't repeat them

You, on the other hand, must focus on: getting out of the financial hole once and for all, learning from your mistakes, and doing whatever it takes to never let it happen again. See yourself as having had financial cancer. It's a disease, you needed major surgery, and you have to adjust expectations for the rest of your life. When you purchased this book, you became eligible for my free *Special Report: The Seven Most Common Money Mistakes People Make and How to Avoid Them*. This report is available at www.GetRealMoney.com\reports.

Beyond all else, focus on getting out of debt, starting with a new set of behaviors and habits. Until you are out of debt, you will feel like debt controls you. Debt will push you around unless you take control of it. You don't get out of debt by playing softball. You've got to play hardball. *You* must make a firm decision because it won't happen unless *you* do. Decide it's up to *you* and that *you* want to become *financially healthy and free*.

Get Real!

Imagine yourself free of debt

Start by getting in touch with the feeling of being financially healthy and financially fit. See yourself smiling and at peace with yourself and those you live with. Close your eyes, breathe deeply, smile, and enjoy that feeling for a minute. It will happen by taking the necessary steps, developing new spending habits, developing and staying with a money plan, and executing the plan faithfully day after day. One thing we teach at every *Get Real! Money Seminar* throughout the United States is setting financial success goals. Thousands of people tell me they have a goal of getting out of debt. That's great, and I applaud them for it, but I don't let them out of it that easily.

I make sure they create a *real* goal and a *real* plan. Without a goal tied to a defined plan, which includes measurable objectives such as a deadline, all you have is a dream. Here's an example of a *real* goal. From here you can create a plan to get results in line with your goal.

Today's date is _____.
　　　　　　　　(actual date you write the goal)
I, _____, have paid off credit card
#_____.

Today's date is _____.
　　　　　　　　(projected completion date)

I feel proud of myself for having delayed gratification
and made the sacrifice to accomplish this goal.

_____.
　　　　　　　　　　(signature)

Get Real!
Set realistic and effective goals for getting out of debt

As you start eliminating your debts, keep in mind that it took you years of poor spending habits to get you where you are now. Eliminating debt will require a serious change in your thinking, and it won't happen overnight. Stick to *The Debt Free Living Action Plan* (see www.GetRealMoney.com) and then reevaluate how it's going. Don't give in, and don't slip back into old habits. It's time to break the debt cycle once and for all.

You are about to break a cycle that may have been in place in your family for generations. The good news is that your decision directly impacts the financial futures of perhaps hundreds of descendants. This is a worthy endeavor to undertake in your life as soon as possible. It will build a healthy financial mentality for success.

Spending money you don't have for items you don't absolutely need is simply a habit. It's a behavior that, until now, you have decided is acceptable. In fact, this trap is what I call being a *money slave*. This habit will eventually catch up with every person and institution that doesn't live within their means—including the United States government. No one can keep adding more and more debt and expect to keep putting off repaying those debts until a sunnier day.

Our national financial policies are a reflection of politicians giving the public exactly what it wants. If politicians give people what they want, people will vote for them—right? These financial policies over the last 75 years have slowly but surely weakened our generation's financial foundation, as well as that of generations to come. Eventually, the house of cards will fall. Be sure to build your house on the foundation of correct proven principles and strategies as outlined in this book. Then, when the wind blows, you'll be left standing while everybody else is caught in the storm!

The question remains: how do I get out of debt if money scarcity was my problem in the first place? Debt develops as a combination of poor thinking, unregulated spending, poor financial habits, and not having the money you want to do the things you want to do.

Once you get your spending under control, then and only then can you be objective, look at options, consolidate debts, create a plan, simplify your lifestyle, and clear your head enough to develop other income streams. Getting out of debt is a combination of following five steps:

The Five Steps to Become Debt-Free

Step 1: Acknowledge your situation.
Step 2: Stop all spending.
Step 3: Commit to the Debt-Free Living Action Plan.
Step 4: Pay yourself first.
Step 5: Live below your means.

You are starting a new venture, and you need a clean slate. Your plan of action will become your new road to travel. There will be temptations and obstacles, but nothing is impossible. I have personally worked with thousands of people who came from the most horrific financial situations and made the commitment to plow through and succeed.

Get Real!

Get a copy of your credit report, learn how to read it, and start the process of repairing your credit

Part of your recovery plan is learning about your personal credit profile. Get a copy of your credit report, learn how to read it, and start repairing it. There will be the obvious details included, and there may well be the unexpected, such as bad debts listed on your report unrelated to you—they just happened to end up on your report. Not only can this be a surprise, it can also be alarming. See www.GetRealMoney.com for where, how, and who to contact to pull your own credit report as well as for tips on credit repair.

If you don't currently have credit problem, you also should pull, read, and understand your credit profile. You may find items you had no idea were there. You must eliminate, update, and/or change any incorrect information. Don't let an unjustified black mark on your credit report blindside you at a crucial time such as when you're trying to rent an apartment or buy a house. The discipline of pulling, reading, and dealing with your credit profile is necessary for those who want control of their financial futures. This isn't something you can leave to a "specialist." Remember, you are the specialist! Also remember, don't be frightened of this step. Learning how to read a credit report is not difficult once you've been through it a few times.

Get Real!
Face the fact—you want more money

It's one thing to budget your income to live within your current means. It's yet another to take your finances to an entirely new level. I've had the privilege of showing thousands of people how to raise their income levels to enjoy life more. How does the person with an average income move to above-average-income levels? Living on a small amount of money isn't as fun as living on a lot of money. Which do you want— less or more? You may as well admit it. If you don't really want to be on a constant budget, live month to month, or not have the time to do things you want to do, then it's time to take it to another level. If you want to travel more, spend more time with loved ones, give more money to the less fortunate—it's time to take it to another level.

The "if I had more money" syndrome is poverty thinking, and it's an excuse. Ask anyone who has money. More money doesn't fix your financial problems. It opens the doors to spending more, and if you aren't on guard, you can get into debt faster and deeper. Newer, faster, and better cars (financed); more expensive, newer furniture (financed); bigger and better houses (financed)—don't equal wealth. They equal just more debt for most people. Poverty thinking is a psychological barrier to financial success, and more money doesn't fix it. It can make it more of the same—debt—just more of it. Now that we have ideas on getting debt under control, we can move on to learning where more money is going to come from.

CHAPTER 9

Get Real! Money Protection: Tax Defense Strategy

I LIKE FREE MONEY, DON'T YOU? One of the most important parts of your *Get Real! Game Plan for 21st Century Success* is understanding how the tax system works and how to *make it work for you rather than against you.* The United States government is waiting for you to take action, use its system to your benefit, and bring more money into your life as fast as possible. As far as I'm concerned, that's free money! The problem is that nobody's going to do it for you. Only you can do it.

Do you know what the single greatest expense in life is? It's not food, shelter, cars, or kids—it's taxes. That's why it's so amazing to me that nobody teaches us much about taxes—except, that is, to fear the tax man. The secret is in knowing the rules, how to play by the rules, and how to play defensively. Your goal needs to be to *keep what is already yours and not pay more than what is absolutely required.* That's where the free money is: using the rules to keep your money in your pocket. Let's begin by keeping in mind how America got its start more than 225 years ago.

You may remember a little war called the American Revolution. This was a war over basic principles that people wanted to secure. Our European ancestors originally came here to freely express their religious beliefs and be free from the rule of a centralized taxing authority. The king and his minions wanted to maintain control of the early settlers, and they did this by forcing people to pay taxes. Unfortunately, much of what was sacrificed and fought for early on has been lost over the last 100 years. Today the average American works until the middle of May just to pay the government. In 1943, our elected representatives determined that the government should get paid *before* the wage earner. This is what we call payroll deductions. In fact, income taxes as we know them today didn't even exist until 1913.

We do receive many wonderful benefits from our tax dollars. We are the safest and most secure nation in the world, and we enjoy unprecedented liberty and freedom, and for this I'm thankful. I'm grateful for those who defend our freedoms and for those who went before us to earn and protect our liberties. However, I believe it's time for average Americans to wake up, smell the coffee, and get in the game with those who understand the game of taxation. Here's a fact of life: The tax code was designed and instituted by people who intended to profit by it. However, the tax code can be used to its fullest by almost everyone at any level in society. There are no hidden advantages that only the elite can play by when it comes to tax law.

That's what I mean by *waking up* and getting with the program. In America, we the taxpayers are *guilty until proven innocent*. I hope the upcoming chapters will inspire you to take action and become a more educated, strategic taxpayer once and for all, so you too can enjoy the many benefits the tax code and its guidelines provide.

Get Real!
Feel privileged about paying your taxes

I want you to feel good about paying your income tax. I personally enjoy paying income tax and view it as a privilege. For me, it's a measurement of financial health. We all have to pay it, and, frankly, the more you pay, the more you must pay attention. It's time to become tax-savvy no matter where you stand financially, because if you intend to have money, prepare now. I'm not suggesting that you become a tax expert or a CPA. I just want you to have a level of comfort, confidence, and mastery so you feel in control in this area of your finances. Keep in mind that when you mail in your tax return, it's your signature on the form—not only the tax preparer's or CPA's. The government will hold you accountable for what's on it.

Remember who makes the rules in the first place. It's the ones with the money who want to maintain control. It's the wealthy who want the middle class kept in line and paying as much as possible. The middle class pay the lion's share of taxes. However, the rich pay a larger percentage of their incomes. Keep in mind that the rich make the rules, they know how to play the game or hire people who do, and they pay as little as possible and are very strategic in doing so.

Get Real!
Make the decision to get in the game and play

Your goal needs to be to get in the game and begin to play the way the successful players do. Yes, I will teach you what you must know to legally reduce your taxes. However, it all starts by making the decision to be in the game. You'll find it's really no secret. It's a matter of using the tax code the way it was designed to be used and developing a working strategy to implement it for your benefit. Now is the time for you to decide to play ball, play by the rules, and learn to love it at the same time. Do as the wealthy do.

Get Real!
Play by the rules

Decide the way you want to play. The best way to play is with a proactive posture that says, "I'm here to play as well as possible, and I play by the rules." You want the money in *your* pocket, not Uncle Sam's. Get in the game and play with a little attitude. Enjoy the game. You'll develop confidence and skill as time goes along, and you'll find more money in your pocket as well. This isn't a game of who wins or loses; it's more a matter of "the one who plays has all the fun." It's as simple as that. There are rules, and when you get in the game and play by them, you've got nothing to worry about.

The fun is in knowing how to use the tax code to your benefit. You need to take control of your tax-paying responsibilities, or they will take control of you. In fact, the government is really hoping you'll let it have total control and you won't play too hard—if at all. The first real step and obstacle that needs to be faced is fear. Too many Americans are frozen in fear of the Internal Revenue Service.

Get Real!
Determine to overcome fear of the IRS by educating yourself

The IRS has trained Americans to be afraid, and many people have fallen into the trap. I want you to know there is nothing to fear. There are rules to play by, and you succeed by playing by the rules. I will never encourage you to do anything illegal, immoral, or unethical. I also recommend that you find a trusted tax advisor you can turn to for counsel. Now, proceed forward by facing the fear you may have. Acknowledge it for what it is. Most fears are unwarranted and based on lack of information and misinformation. It's time to get the necessary education and develop it into confidence.

The way to begin is to use the rulebook. It's called the U.S.

Tax Code. It's in English and you can understand it. When you get stumped, find somebody who understands it and ask him or her—that's what your tax advisor is for.

It's important for you to accept and play by the rules, because this is not your ballpark. You didn't make the rules, and you won't be changing them any time soon. Accept the rules, embrace them, study them, and use them the way they are meant to be used. I do not want you to become a "tax expert." What I do want is for you to have a working knowledge of the rules so you can play well. There is a right time to hire an expert, and this is one of them. Hiring a good tax advisor will give you the time to focus on the activities you do best. Knowing who you want on your team, how you expect them to play, and educating yourself on the rules of the game are the keys to your success.

Get Real!
Always use tax strategies, never loopholes or tax cheating

Isn't it nice to know that legitimate, legal, and ethical tax strategies are made equally available to everyone? They're not reserved for the chosen few. You will never need to cheat or break laws to have access to tax strategies that can save you large amounts of money every year.

As you proceed, I want you to make the distinction between a tax strategy and a loophole. In my view, a strategy is a straightforward interpretation of the written code, whereas a loophole falls within the "gray area" of interpretation.

Whenever I hear the term "loophole" from someone, I'm cautious. I'm teaching you to use well-documented, proven techniques that are without question on the up and up. A loophole is something not yet well defined. The tax code, to a large degree, has many black-and-white instructions. However, there is a significant area not well defined. This gray area is where the loopholes come in. Many times it's the gray area that causes problems, and this is the area you want to avoid. Let's just get a solid working plan for using absolute black-and-white strategies and leave the loopholes for those who want to play that game.

Get Real!
Reduce your taxes legally by following IRS rules and guidelines

There is a right way and a wrong way to begin reducing your taxes. The right way is to do it properly by following the rules and guidelines in the tax code. The wrong way is to stretch a reasonable interpretation of the code to the point of being unreasonable or flat-out wrong.

I encourage you to firmly decide to stick to an unwavering principle that you pay any and all taxes owed to the IRS. Simply get used to the process, and in turn, this will help force you to better understand how to use strategies for properly cutting taxes with the tax code. Remember, successful people don't know it all; they just know who does.

Someone once called Henry Ford an uneducated man, not having made it past the sixth grade. The story goes that the successful automaker told the man, "You can take everything away I have accomplished and have accumulated and I will have it all back in two years—just leave me my telephone."

There's the secret to his success. He surrounded himself with competent people he trusted, people he liked and felt would be good team players. You, too, don't need to know it all—you just need to know who does. Notice that it's not necessarily the people who are the technical experts in their field who have the money. It's the people who use resource people who are smarter than themselves and put them to work to their benefit.

Get Real!
Find a competent, trustworthy, and friendly tax advisor

The next question is: how do I find the right tax advisor? This comes back to learning how to build a team of professionals who can support you properly over time. You must have a working strategy for picking and choosing the people you want to associate with. It's your ballpark this time. You choose the players, you interview them, and you must know what to look for. Let's look at what makes a good tax advisor.

Choose someone who is in the game. Once tax advisors have established themselves professionally, which may take years, they may specialize in one area of their field. For instance, some tax advisors specialize in cranking out tax returns as fast as possible. Some specialize in providing strategic financial advice. Some specialize in working with small businesses, while others deal with large corporations.

You will pay almost the same money for a professional who is brand new in the business as someone who has twenty-five years of experience in an area of specialization. My advice is to hire people who are seasoned in their fields. There's no way you can replace years and years of practical application. That's how and why experts become experts.

Get Real!
Start a library of basic tax reference materials

One of your first action steps will be to visit www.GetRealMoney.com\resources, where you'll locate the various government tax publications. These are "pdf" files you can easily view using Adobe Acrobat Reader. These standard publications are what tax advisors refer to, and they should be part of your reference library. When you have a question, you can develop confidence in finding the answer by getting comfortable with these publications. If you still have a question once you've reviewed the publication, contact your tax advisor to confirm your understanding and ask for his or her *opinion*. Always remember, when you receive an *opinion* from a licensed professional, it's only that, an opinion. They interpret the code based on their experience of how case law has interpreted the tax code as it applies to the question you have. It's important that you begin to develop a *feel* for how a good advisor interprets tax code so you can develop your own confidence level.

Please remember, you are capable and don't need to exclusively rely on a third party for all information at all times. This is about stepping up to the plate because you want more money in your life—right? Your signature on your tax forms is still your signature, and you are responsible for it, not a tax advisor. Tax advisors are paid to give you the best information they can, based on their professional experience and the information you have provided. Nobody knows more or cares more about your finances than you. Never forget that!

Get Real!
Trust your own ability and develop confidence

I want you to tap into as much free support, help, and literature as possible. I suggest you take advantage of it all. Remember, when asking tax-related questions of the IRS over the phone, IRS representatives have been known to give inaccurate information at times. They do the best they can. However, you must always review tax publication documents yourself. IRS representatives will always reference documents for you and ask if you would like them sent to you. This protects them, because it's understood that they are not tax advisors; they are reading the same document you can access and read.

Trust your own abilities. Do not be afraid of reading and understanding tax publications. Realize that with time and education you can handle this. Paying taxes is a fact of life, and those who understand and utilize the tax code for their benefit are the ones with the money. If you want money in your life, you must view your taxes differently than you have in the past.

Get Real!
Understand your tax return

It's absolutely necessary to learn how to read your tax return to build your financial self-confidence. This is a healthy thing to do, and I recommend that you not let another year go by without doing it. Understand how to read your own tax return *before* you mail it in. Take out a recent return and study it, page by page. Begin to familiarize yourself with the forms and schedules. Ask a knowledgeable advisor for answers in order to get comfortable. You want to know what your tax return consists of so you have better control of what you are doing. Don't be afraid of it—just ask good questions of smart people who can help you.

Your tax plan begins by taking full advantage of all itemized deductions on Schedule A. Schedule A is a simple two-page form attached to Form 1040A. Be sure to take all deductions you are entitled to: medical/dental expenses; home mortgage interest; gifts to charity; unreimbursed employee expenses such as job travel, union dues, and job education; tax preparation fees; and other permitted miscellaneous deductions.

Get Real!
Construct a tax plan using proven tax strategies

Once you understand your tax return, it's time to develop a *tax plan* using proven tax strategies. Creating a workable and strategic tax plan is an absolute necessity for your financial success. If you don't plan, you'll end up spending more on taxes than you should. When you begin receiving your *FREE Special Gift Subscription* to the *Get Real! Money News*, you will learn many other valuable tax strategies.

You *build into your tax plan* strategies that give you the flexibility you'll need. For example, the top tax-savings strategy is operating and running a small business either part-time or full-time. By having a small business, you open the doors to deductions you otherwise wouldn't have. "We have two tax systems in the United States," tax law specialist Sandy Botkin explains. "One system is for employees and for those that don't know the rules. This system is designed to take your wealth. The second tax system is for the self-employed people who know the rules. This system is designed to create economic growth."[1]

I've covered the most powerful tax strategies of all— free enterprise and real estate—in upcoming chapters. But before we look at them, and now that you have a better understanding of how taxation plays a role in your financial success, it's time to learn how having an investment strategy also plays a major role in your *Get Real! Game Plan for 21st Century Success.*

---

1. Sandy Botkin, *Lower Your Taxes—Big Time* (McGraw-Hill, 2003).

CHAPTER 10

Get Real! Money for Life: Investment Strategy

THINK BACK FOR JUST A MINUTE about what you were taught throughout your kindergarten through twelfth grade education—*get ready to work for the rest of your life for someone else.* For twelve years, we were prepared for it and trained to expect it. Do you remember anyone even mentioning the idea of owning and operating a business? Our entire educational system is still geared to teaching people to get a job working for someone else. This is a 20th century mind-set that I call *trading time for dollars.* In this chapter, I show you *how to make money work for you—so you don't work for it.* It all begins by challenging the trading-time-for-dollars thinking we grew up with.

We were trained to trade an hour of time and effort for a wage, or to trade a year of time and effort for a salary. The problem is that there are only so many hours in a day, a week, a month, or a year a person can work. You must learn the secret of *leveraging your time* if you want above-average income and long-term permanent income.

Mom and Dad never knew how or what to teach us to earn an above-average income. What we weren't told was that there are other types of income you must know about if you want above-average money:

1. Earned income—working for others/working for yourself

2. Passive income—real estate investments

3. Investment or portfolio income—stocks and bonds

In the next chapters, you'll learn the secrets of all three—why you need them and how to begin generating them to begin making money work for you, so you don't have to work forever for your money.

The late financial educator, Charles J. Givens, said in his book, *Wealth Without Risk*, that there are five ways of making money:[1]

1. Putting yourself to work—employment

2. Putting other people to work—business

3. Putting your ideas to work—inventing, marketing, or consulting

4. Putting your money to work—investing

5. Putting other people's money to work—leverage

To keep it simple—*people make money, or money makes money.* In some way, shape, or form, it's trading time for dollars (people make money) or a form of leverage (money makes money). We were trained in only the first—people make money. You can leverage your time, your ideas, and other people's knowledge, as well as other people's efforts, to create wealth for yourself.

---

1. Charles J. Givens, *Wealth Without Risk* (Simon & Schuster, 1991).

If you don't, you'll be stuck in the financial rat race of trying to create money one way—trading your time and effort. As you well know, you eventually wear out. You can only work so much in a day, and you don't want to always be on the treadmill. You want to get off and relax, right? So let's learn to begin *leveraging* your smarts and further develop your money muscles.

Get Real!
Get leverage on your time and money

To have the free time and the money to do what you want, you will need to know the concept of *investing* money versus just *earning* and *spending* money. What is investing, how do I invest, and where do I invest? I want you to have the experience of seeing and participating in the process of watching *your* money compound. A key to developing leverage is learning and developing *new habits*. We discussed the first and most important habit of success in a previous chapter. It's the habit of delayed gratification—putting off something today for a desirable result you want in the future.

Get Real!
Invest versus spend

Investing time, money, and effort versus spending time, money, and effort is in the way we *think*. If you really want money to work for you, rather than you always having to work for it, you must *invest* time, effort, and money now in order to get what you want in the future. Notice the word—*invest*. It's time to begin delaying activities you'd rather be doing now, the places you'd rather go now, and the money you'd rather spend now—for future benefits.

Again, you'll need to eliminate old habits and learn new ones. For example, *spending all* you earn is a habit. *Spending more* than you have is a habit. *Watching too much television* is a habit. *Eating out* too often is a habit. We form habits over time without even knowing it. The results of these habits leave you not having the money to do the things you want when you want to do them. Our society has formed a habit of the exact opposite of delayed gratification. It's called *instant gratification.*

When I say the word "investing," I know what may have gone through your mind. You may have said something like "I'm not capable of investing. I don't know how, I don't have money, and I'm not smart enough." Get real—these are all excuses.

You are capable of becoming your own best financial manager, and now's your chance. You don't need someone else doing it for you. You can learn proven strategies and stick to a plan, and you can start right where you are. If you don't take financial matters into your own hands, there is always somebody else who will be glad to manage it for you—for a part of the pie.

Get Real!
Become your own best financial manager

Any time you ask someone else to manage your money or to create plans for you, you're going to pay for it in more ways than one. It's time to become your own best money manager, your own investment advisor, and your own financial planner. At some point, you may choose to hire a financial advisor/ financial planner, but do it only after you are experienced and prepared to manage that person. First, learn to become your own best financial manager and then you will be better positioned to hire a financial advisor/planner. Also, never hire a commission-paid financial planner/advisor unless you have the utmost trust that he or she is looking out for your best interests and not only his or hers.

Remember, the majority of Americans are virtually broke in ninety days or less if they lose their jobs. It's because they've been managing their money the way their employers require them to do it, the way the government has taught them to do it, and the way their parents showed them how to do it. If you continue to operate the old way, you continue to get the same results.

Get Real!
Come to grips with any fears about your ability to be your own best financial manager

Begin by facing any fears you may have about handling money and the idea of investing. Have you ever heard yourself say something like "I can't understand investing," or "I can't do it without money"? The best way to start investing is to acknowledge you may be dealing with fear regarding being an investor. Once you admit it, you take away the power it has over you. It's like looking into the eye of a bully and realizing he's been trying to intimidate you and scare you into submission.

If it makes you feel any better, many Americans are afraid of investing. Once you come to terms with any fears, you can begin a strategic plan of attack. I've found that most fears are caused by a lack of information in a particular area. Once you acknowledge fear, you can get new information, which can be used to build a knowledge base. Then you can take action, which will build your self-confidence, which results in success, which develops a feeling of positive self-mastery. We move from fear to self-mastery through this process.

The Five Steps to Break Through Financial Fears

Step 1: Acknowledge fear for what it is.

Step 2: Acquire specialized knowledge.

Step 3: Take action.

Step 4: Build confidence.

Step 5: Experience success and self-mastery.

Get Real!
Start investing now—not later

In a previous chapter, I mentioned how I started investing with $1,000. Well, I could have started with $1 and started even sooner. Think back to what you were taught as a child about investing. Put your money in the savings account and it will be safe. That's it! That's all our parents knew. That's what they learned from their parents and from the bank. If you came from a sophisticated home, you read the newspaper and it taught you how to invest, right? Well, the newspaper is filled with _old_ news, and the people in the game are the ones who create the news and _control_ the money. As we move on, I'll show you ways of receiving from 10 to 1,000 percent rates of return on your investment. For now, I just want you to start! Start now, start small, and begin with whatever you can. It's time to develop a _habit_ of investing for the long term. These simple habits are what separate the rich from the poor in America. See www.GetRealMoney.com under Investing.

Get Real!
Invest in yourself and your ongoing financial education

Investing in your personal growth and development will give you the highest returns of any investment you can possibly make. Reading this book and applying what you are learning is an investment of time. Go to seminars, read books, and listen to tapes and CDs that will improve your life. A tremendous investment is to attend a _Get Real! Money Seminar_ as soon as possible.

Get Real!

Be careful where you get your information— avoid the investment myths trap

One of the most common investment myths is that to receive significant rates of return on an investment, you will need to take big risks. That's what we're taught, right? Well, that's not the truth. More risk doesn't always equal more reward, and large rewards don't always involve taking big risks. That type of inaccurate information will keep many people from investing. It's not only a matter of getting new information; it's about getting *good information* that moves us from fear to success.

Get Real!

Plan on eliminating unnecessary financial risks you are already taking

I want you to develop wealth by taking as little risk as possible. Eliminate the risks you already take that may be hurting you without your even knowing it. Here's the single greatest financial risk most people in America choose to take—working exclusively for someone else! Putting your financial life in someone else's complete control is a huge risk that you can quickly reduce. This is why I emphasize in this book two specific areas for investment: free enterprise and real estate, both of which give you control and reduce risk.

Here's the other major risk most people are taking with their money—they risk their financial futures with their lack of knowledge regarding money. That's highly risky. Learning about and understanding money is risk-free.

Get Real!

Understand diversification

The next investment strategy is known as *diversification*. Most people refer to diversification in terms of diversifying a portfolio of stocks and bonds, which is, in part, correct and, in part, poor advice.

I believe in diversification for safety first and foremost. That's why I'll suggest a mutual fund for most people before individual stocks, because a mutual fund is a large, diverse group of stocks/bonds. If any one of the individual stocks or bonds doesn't do well, it pulls down the overall value of the entire fund, but the result is not as significant as having owned that one stock or bond alone. I'll discuss more about this later.

Get Real!
Don't own stocks and bonds at the same time

Many people are also taught to diversify a portfolio of both stocks and bonds by what some call *balancing*. This concept is questionable at best. If you look at the past history of bond values, the overall return is in direct contradiction to the overall returns generated in the stock market. When stock values rise, bonds historically have fallen, and vice versa. Investment values are significantly driven by interest rates. When interest rates are lower, businesses can expand and create more value faster. This creates more profits, which then directly impacts the value of the stock in the marketplace.

Historically, our economy runs in cycles of a two- to three-year recession, followed by a six- to eight-year expansion. We are quickly becoming a globally driven economy that is affected by worldwide trade and worldwide markets, but the basic principle of balancing still doesn't create safety. When interest rates are rising, bond values decrease. When interest rates are declining, bond values rise. Typically bond values will depreciate 10 percent for every 1 percent rise in prime interest rate. Conversely, bond values will appreciate 10 percent for every 1 percent drop in interest prime rate. When interest rates are within an acceptable range (4–9 percent), stocks historically have done well. When interest rates go below a certain threshold (6 percent), bonds historically haven't performed well. When bond funds aren't performing, money will flow out of bonds and into stocks, causing stock prices to rise. It also works the other way around. Always invest with the following in mind.

> ## The Three Master Strategies of Successful Investors
>
> **Strategy 1:** Investment value goes up and down based on the market (buyers and sellers). If nobody wants to buy, prices go down. If everybody wants to buy, prices go up.
>
> **Strategy 2:** Current investment value is affected by external factors you can't control. For example, the public may start selling stocks because of some uncontrollable factor such as news of war, the economy, or the weather. Then the herd follows. When the herd follows, suddenly there are more sellers than buyers, which in turn, drives down the prices people are willing to pay. The real winners are the ones who buy when the market is low and sell when it's high.
>
> **Strategy 3:** Investment values are not based solely on intrinsic value, because of the above factors. An investment holds a current market value primarily based on fluctuations of supply and demand in an active marketplace. The supply and demand of Wall Street is often driven by emotion, not logic.

Get Real!
Cut your losses short and run your winners long

One of the most difficult parts of investing is being able to make logical, nonemotional investment decisions well. Too often people hang on to an investment that they hope and pray and believe is going to revive or magically recover, even though it's lost steam.

Hoping or praying for a miracle in this area is not a winning financial strategy. The best thing to do is to simply cut your loss as fast as possible and move on. Don't hang on hoping the investment's going to come back—it probably won't, period. Your money can be better invested elsewhere and not losing value. The opposite is also true: hang on to the winners and ride them as long as they're winning. Just keep in mind, that most investments have their own time and life. Your job is to know enough about what you are doing in order to make qualified buy/sell decisions.

There are, clearly, certain types of investments and investment strategies you want to begin using right away. For example, in upcoming sections of this book, I'll discuss the power of real estate investing and why real estate investment and operating a small business are the best investments you can make.

Get Real!

Get your current investment portfolio in order and put it to best use

First, if you have current investment accounts such as IRAs, SEP-IRAs, Roth IRAs, or a 401(k) from a company where you previously worked, put these to the best use. I want you to direct where the money is invested and in what type of investments. This is called *self-directed investing*. Any IRA or 401(k) from a previous employer can be self-directed. You may need to transfer money from one or several accounts to a self-directed trustee provider so you have *full control* over directing what is to be done with it, including purchasing investment real estate.

Get Real!

Use the self-directed investment approach

It is important to consolidate all the accounts you may have. It can be a challenge making the arrangements, but you must do it, or else your investment accounts may be with several different trustees and difficult to manage.

The Six Steps to Getting Your Investments Under Control

Step 1: Make a list of every current account you have, what the account numbers are, what they're currently invested in, and the phone numbers of the current trustees.

Step 2: Choose a trustee for self-directed investing. See www.GetRealMoney.com under Investing.

Step 3: Consolidate as much as possible to one trustee. This means combining perhaps several IRAs you may have into one account. Companies charge individual fees for each entity account, and this will save service fees.

Step 4: Choose the investment you want the money invested in.

Step 5: Direct the trustee to make the investment for you.

Step 6: Mark your calendar to check the account every three to six months for performance.

Most retirement accounts are tax-deferred, which means the growth of principle is not taxable until you take a distribution. A distribution occurs only when you permanently take the money out. Currently you are not required to take the money out until you are 70½ years old. When you do take a distribution, taxes will be payable then. The current exception to this rule is the Roth IRA. It is initially funded with after-taxed dollars. The capital appreciation of a Roth IRA is not subject to a capital gains tax or an income tax under current tax law.

If you do take a distribution before the allowed time (59½ years old) and don't put it back within sixty calendar days, this would be considered a taxable distribution. Also, on top of capital gains tax, a 10 percent penalty will be charged for an early distribution. There are exemptions for medical emergencies, as well as for the use for a down payment on a first home.

Investing properly is the key to making money work for you—so you don't work for it. This is how you put in place a long-term solution so that someday you won't have to work unless you want to. Now I'll show you the absolute best investments you can ever make.

CHAPTER 11

**Master Money
Strategy #4**

Get Real! Money Security:
Free Enterprise Strategy

THE BEST JOB IN THE WORLD IS one in which
you get to work when you want, with whom you
want, where you want, and make as much as you
want. There's only one place you'll ever get that
job, and that's by working for yourself through free
enterprise. Learning how to become successfully
self-employed will eventually help you to reduce
stress and live a healthier, happier, and longer life.
The ultimate way to achieve career success is by
applying Master Money Strategy #4: *Free Enterprise
Strategy*.

By far the best place to invest is to invest in yourself and your future by owning a small business/
personal enterprise and by owning real estate. At
every *Get Real! Money Seminar* I teach, I encourage
every participant to decide to become his or her own
boss, either part-time or full-time, even if he or she
has a job. If you have a job and are happy with the

way you're treated, have the time flexibility you want, and are getting paid well—keep it, it's a great form of cash flow. Be thankful you are one of the few who actually have this going for them. However, you must begin generating other income on the side by building a small business or investing in real estate in order to create a safety zone in case you end up not having that cash flow some day.

Here's a list of the benefits of being self-employed part-time or full-time:

> ### The Five Major Benefits of Self-Employment
>
> 1. Income potential—no glass ceiling
> 2. Time freedom and flexibility
> 3. Tax advantages
> 4. Choice of people you work with
> 5. Financial safety and security

Get Real!

If you want financial safety and security, be your own boss at least part-time

The most important benefit is number 5: *financial safety and security*. Today people want safety and security more than almost anything. If you want financial safety and security, invest the time, money, and effort in developing your ability to be successfully self-employed least on a part-time basis alongside your other work. Self-employment skills produce money for you. Without them, it's virtually impossible to become financially independent in the 21st century. For most people, working a regular job will mean a paycheck-to-paycheck lifestyle forever. It is almost impossible to become financially secure by working a forty- to fifty-hour week for someone else.

By having a business or real estate that provides another form of cash flow, you are limiting your financial risks by not depending on only one income stream—thus creating safety for yourself. Jobs and businesses have seasons—winter, spring, summer, and fall. By diversifying your sources of cash flow, you enter the *cash flow safety zone*. When winter comes, you will have protected yourself by having developed multiple sources of cash flow.

Get Real!
Start a small business part-time or full-time

Our world has changed. It's no longer smart to put your eggs in one basket—either one job or one business. The "I'll find myself a big company and stay there for forty years" game doesn't exist any more. People are increasingly frustrated with companies that have no interest in employing people past fifty years of age, paying for retirements, or giving lifelong benefits. The traditional model of employment has permanently changed, never to be the same as it was years ago. Unfortunately, millions of hard-working, smart Americans are only now just waking up to the facts.

You may already own a business or two, but have never really considered developing your skills to be able to become even more successful and profitable in business. Many business owners I work with—and I work with thousands—start businesses and just get caught up in them. They wake up years later finding that the business has been running *them*. They worked *in* their business, but didn't work *on* their business.

Get Real!
Develop your own Business Blueprint™

The way to begin solving this problem, as well as to how to determine what might be a good business venture for you, is to first create a *Business Blueprint*. The *Business Blueprint* is a snapshot of the ultimate business, customized to your personal goals, talents, and desires. If you could have your dream business, what would it be like? I've created what I believe to be the perfect scenario in the *Business Blueprint*, and you can build your own customized *Business Blueprint* at www.GetRealMoney.com under the Small Business section. It's simple—you just click on the attributes you want to include and you can then use this as a guideline for choosing which business venture may be right for you. We've even included suggestions that may fit your profile. If you are currently in business, take a minute to build one, too. You'll find it helpful in keeping you on track as you continue to grow. Keep in mind that it takes time to actually develop this business. The *Business Blueprint* is used as the destination point of your business growth.

The problem with many business owners is that they start a business and have some success—just enough to keep them working for themselves but many times not experiencing the lifestyle they really wanted. When they wake up, they ask themselves, "How in the world did I end up here?" Good question to be asking—wrong time to be asking it!

Get Real!
Get a life—not a business!

Having a business and being self-employed should become much more than just working for yourself. I want you to *get a life!* Here's what I mean. Many people start careers and businesses the exact same way—they have good intentions, they work hard, and they do their best to stay focused. In fact, we stay so focused that we forget the reasons we're doing it in the first place.

We get off target by making our process of generating income (the business or career) the means *and* the end. We forget that it's about having a life that's most important, not only making money. As you make the effort to build a business, don't get caught in the trap most people do when building a career or a business. Make building the business just one aspect of your life, not your entire life. If you're already a business owner, you probably know exactly what I'm talking about. A business can take on a life of its own and can start talking to you, saying things like:

- Hey, over here, where do you think you're going? You're not done yet.

- Hey, you, you should be fixing me now, not spending time with your family.

- Wait, don't leave; I want just one more thing.

- I'm having a crisis; you can't take a vacation; get back here.

- You exist for me, not me for you—remember that.

It can be like a little child who plays helpless. You control it, or it will demand control of you. The secret is in knowing how to turn it off, how to control it, and how to say no.

Get Real!
Follow your customized Business Blueprint

Today, 80 percent of small business owners launch businesses and remain slightly off track by not following a blueprint. They wonder how they ended up where they did—they either didn't have a Business Blueprint to begin with or they didn't stick to it.

> Create a Business Blueprint ➡
> Correct and adjust ➡
> Stay on track

They ended up with a business, but not a life. There was little planned time for evaluation and making the necessary corrections and adjustments. They were so busy running the business that it ended up running them. This scenario is common today in small business. I've seen it thousands of times with the people I've personally worked with. I, too, made the same mistake, and that's why I'm encouraging you not to.

Get Real!

Discover exactly what business is best for you

It can be challenging to discover exactly what business is best for you. The secret is in knowing what you want in a business before you start and then staying on track using a blueprint. One excellent way to discover what business will be good for you is by identifying exactly what you know you *do not want*. Doing this will help you identify the opposite—what you really *do* want. Here's a list of the businesses you definitely don't want. You may have had one of them, perhaps you can add a few:

> The *"Make-No-Money Business"* ➡
>   I want a business that is profitable.
>
> The *"I-Don't-Have-a-Life Business"* ➡
>   I want a life, not merely a business.
>
> The *"I-Have-No-Friends-Left Business"* ➡
>   I want to enjoy the people I'm working with,
>   and want to create new relationships
>   through my business.
>
> The *"I-Never-Get-a-Vacation Business"* ➡
>   I want to be able to travel four times a year
>   for ten days each.
>
> The *"I-Hate-Myself Business"* or
> the *"I'm-Not-Myself Business"* ➡
>   I want to look, act, and feel great about
>   myself.

These are the results many business owners get because they don't think like an entrepreneur. We must get you on the right track from the beginning.

Get Real!

If you currently own a business and are off track, get back on track

We find ourselves off track all the time. Correct and adjust quickly, not slowly. If you're headed for the North Pole but want to go to New York, get back on track now. Take the short route. You don't have to backtrack; get back on *the* track, which is defined by your *Business Blueprint*.

At our *Get Real! Money Seminars* we specialize in training beginners and seasoned professionals on how to either begin on the right track or to get back on track for those already in business.

Get Real!

Work *on* your business—not only *in* your business

Many business owners back themselves into the corner of becoming a *technician* within the business rather than the *entrepreneur* working on the business. They let the business run *them*, rather than running the business. Businesses take on a life of their own and will eat you alive if you aren't careful. Before you launch your business, or grow your business to the next level, make sure you don't end up with a job working for yourself. Unfortunately, that's exactly what 90 percent of American business owners do. I had one business for ten years. I worked day and night. One day I decided it was time for me to move on, so I tried to sell it. Guess what—nobody wanted to buy it, because I didn't go with it. After ten years of blood, sweat, and tears, I realized I had run a business with zero value other than the real estate I owned. It was a difficult lesson to learn, and one I will not repeat.

Get Real!
Decide "why" you want to have your own business

Why should you start or own a business? Because it's worth it! I never said working for yourself was easy. It's simple, but it's not easy. It's invigorating running a business. Not only do you create a financial safety structure, but you're also putting a higher value on yourself. It feels great being in charge, knowing you choose the price to put on your efforts.

Ask anyone you know who's self-employed. He or she reached a point in the process where it was time to say, "I'm not turning back; it's got its challenges, but nobody will ever pay me what I know I'm worth." I call it the great "turning point." It's that magical point when you've reached a sense of destiny, a commitment to the fact that you can and will forever remain—the boss.

I realize that not everybody is a born leader of people, or wants to be the boss. That's why you must do some soul-searching and decide—do I want to have financial freedom or not? If you do, you must pay the price, develop the skill, take the bull by the horns, and find your place developing additional income working for yourself. There's a place for everyone, especially once you learn how to make the business fit you, your personality, and your desires. We're not born with the talent of operating businesses. Everyone has to commit to developing the skills, getting the know-how, and sharpening their abilities. Not only can you develop permanent career security through free enterprise, and design exactly what you want it to look like by blueprinting, you can also determine exactly what you want your enterprise to do for you.

CHAPTER 12

How to Get the Best Job in the World

CONSIDER THE OPPORTUNITY IN AMERICA for free enterprise as *your* opportunity to have the best job in the world! Your personal enterprise will become what *you* make of it and what *you* want it to be. In effect, you have the opportunity to *create* the job of your dreams. That's right; you decide how you will operate, when you will work, who you will work with, and what you will do to perform your work. That's freedom, and certainly the best job in the world! Even though working for yourself is the best work in the world, some people are reluctant to commit to free enterprise because of a few misconceptions. These are easy to deal with, and we'll do just that in this chapter, starting with receiving a benefit package from your employer.

Most people think the only way to have a business is to work full-time at it. Not true! Keep in mind, you can begin and grow a personal enterprise on the side of a regular job. You don't have to give up a benefits package until you feel you are ready.

Get Real!

Develop and manage your own benefits package

What are the benefits you receive working for others? It comes down to a steady paycheck of after-tax dollars, a health plan, and, maybe, if you're lucky, a retirement benefit. Remember, most health plans aren't portable. Today we must be the ones managing our own benefit packages, or we're letting someone else take care of us. Letting someone else manage your benefits package for you is a major risk and can result in financial devastation if and when the benefits no longer exist. We are seeing more and more people falling through the cracks, not being able to maintain consistent health coverage, moving from job to job. Visit www.GetRealMoney.com under Small Business for helpful information on starting a benefits package for yourself, including health insurance and retirement accounts.

When we work for ourselves, we have a totally new opportunity. We have the opportunity to provide valuable products and services that meet the wants and needs of our customers and clients. New ideas are driving this new-world economy, and there has never been a better time or opportunity in history to be self-employed part-time or full-time.

Everybody can afford to start a small business offering products or services on the side, even after they've worked a full-time job. Many people believe that if they need more money, they should get another job—trading time for dollars. Free enterprise is about beginning to create leverage in your life. When you trade your time for dollars, you give your most valuable resource away—your time! You surrender control to someone else's wealth-building purposes, and they get all the benefits. I'm suggesting that you put yourself to work as your first employee, with four to ten hours per week of effort.

Get Real!
Don't put it off—start now, not later

Once you start, you'll look back and say you wish you had done this years ago. Many times in my seminars I take time to answer people's personal questions in small groups. I've had younger people ask me if they should start a business. I'll ask the older ones in the group, "What do you think he or she should do?" They all respond the same way: Do it now, and don't wait like I did—get going, now's the time, take action. This is your life we're talking about, not a casual thing to invest. Invest it wisely, with care, skill, tact, and strategy.

Get Real!
The Exit Strategy™

When you own your business, you are building long-term security for yourself. An enterprise should eventually become a financial equity for you that is salable. It must be developed properly by designing a set of processes called business systems. If done properly, you'll not just have a business, but an *equity with a marketable value that can later be sold for a profit.* As part of your overall business planning, plan now to eventually sell your business. This is called an Exit Strategy. Imagine having a job making $40,000 per year. Let's say you don't want to work there any longer. If it was your business, you should be able to sell that position for five to ten times your net earnings. Imagine selling your job for $200,000 to $400,000. That's what I mean when I say building a business is about building a salable equity. Businesses are bought and sold all the time, just like real estate. If done correctly, the sale of your business now can become a recurring income for you for years to come.

Operating your own business can also be a tremendous creative outlet. I'm a creative person and have found business to be a great outlet for my creativity, because I work *on* my businesses. I enjoy the creative pursuit of developing new marketing techniques, as well as products and services. I need a creative outlet, and this gives me a place to be creative on a regular basis. Good business is first and foremost about knowing how to effectively serve people.

Get Real!
Decide to enjoy working with people to bring more money into your life

One of the great benefits of creating the best job in the world is that it involves people. If you enjoy people, start a business. If you feel you really don't like people, you can learn—with practice and commitment—to enjoy people. Developing your skill in dealing with the public will make you a lot of money. If money is what you want, learn to be effective with people. Working with people is one of my favorite aspects of business. I thoroughly enjoy exploring what they want, what makes them tick, what products and services they want, and why they want them. I enjoy giving people what they want, and I enjoy making a profit by doing so.

Get Real!
Let Uncle Sam subsidize your financial life by running a small business

Another reason to create the best job in the world, either part-time or full-time, is that Uncle Sam wants to give you money to do so. We've discussed the phenomenal tax incentives that are available only to those operating a business. When you start a business, you generate taxable income for the government. As you employ people, you create even more taxable income for the government. The government always gets paid before the employee, through payroll deductions. When jobs are created, people have money to spend on other taxable items, creating the merry-go-round of taxes for local, state, and federal governments.

Small business (which is defined by the IRS as having $4 million or less per year in revenue) creates more new jobs than the large business sector does. Seventy-six percent of all new jobs are created by small businesses with twenty-five or fewer employees. Our government understands this and provides special incentives through grants, loans, and subsidies to support small businesses that stimulate the economy and create new jobs. Visit www.GetRealMoney.com under Small Business for more details on government grants, loans, and subsidies.

Get Real!
Face your fears about being self-employed

Do you have an issue or fear that blocks your launch of a part-time small business? Remember, fear is just an excuse; it's a bully that stands up and keeps you from doing what you want to do. You've got to deal with feelings of fear and break through by doing it anyway. You will feel uncertain at times. Even seasoned business people do, but you need to keep on plowing through. That's how we do it—*we do it in spite of what we feel.*

As mentioned in a previous chapter, the key to breaking through fears is to acknowledge the fear exists, get new information, develop knowledge, take action with that knowledge, create confidence, and experience success and mastery.

I've personally found myself many times experiencing fear and a lack of self-confidence. When I do, I know I'm onto something good. I've learned to be a person who takes action, and when I do, I create momentum, which sooner or later creates success and causes me to feel good about myself.

That's not to say that all experiences are always successful. You may have launched a business and, at some point, not done well. You may consider it a failure. You may consider *yourself* a failure. That's certainly one way to look at it, but don't do that to yourself. Consider the failed venture a great learning experience. Think about what you learned from the experience and what you will make sure to do differently next time. Make good notes about what you learned in your experience equity journal, and be sure to reread that journal every six months. All successful entrepreneurs have fallen many times, including me. The only difference between us and people who are failures is we got back up and kept going. In the real world of self-employment, it's an ongoing process that never ends. The same holds true for the American job, doesn't it? It is really no different except that you are building something for your future that you control and from which you gain the entire benefit.

Get Real!
Jump at the opportunity in America— it has never been better

Opportunity for small business has never been better in America. Imagine yourself at this very moment sitting in your yacht, grilling dinner on the back deck, watching the sunset. The yacht sleeps four, has a full kitchen, and offers a well-designed dining area. You have your favorite drink in one hand and are turning on your favorite music CD with the other. At the same time as the sun is setting over the water and the waves are quietly lapping against the boat, you're running a world-wide business from a laptop computer hooked up to a cell phone! That's what's possible in America today. Unprecedented opportunity exists like never before!

I recently visited an estate of one of the wealthiest business owners in America of the late 19th century. We toured his mansion, including his home office. It was an eight-by-ten-foot room with no air-conditioning, no heat, no electricity, and no running water. Today, beginning business owners have more than he did in his day. I visited Henry Ford's second home in Fort Myers, Florida. I noticed that he didn't even have a closed-in garage! Thomas Edison's summer home office/laboratory had no air-conditioning and no frills. We've got it made in America. It's never been so good! In fact, it's so good that most people don't even recognize it when it's right in front of them.

Get Real!
Look, act, and feel the way you want

When you create the best job in the world working for yourself, you get to look, act, and feel the way you want. At one of my seminars recently, there were two men sitting in the front row eagerly listening to everything I said. Picture this: They each had long gray hair tied back in a ponytail and wore sleeveless black t-shirts. Their burly arms were tattooed from shoulder to fist. I asked them what they did for business. They explained that they purchase motorcycle parts by phone and through the Internet from sellers all over the world. They reassemble bikes in their shop and sell them as collector items to wannabe bikers. Wow!

These dudes are the living dream of successful self-employment. They looked, acted, and felt the way *they* wanted to—not what somebody else wanted. They are true to themselves. The late Mary Kay Ash of Mary Kay Cosmetics fame is another good example of this. She inspired millions of women to look, act, and feel great about themselves, as well as giving them the opportunity to become businesswomen. She not only helped these women look, act, and feel good about themselves, she also taught them to celebrate it. In both examples, these people created businesses where they could truly express themselves in a way they chose. Now that's exciting!

Get Real!
Travel the world as part of your business and make it tax deductible

One of the most overlooked and most exciting tax deductions is your travel. I love to travel, but I love tax-deductible business-related travel even more. Look for ways to combine your recreational travel with legitimate business activities so a portion of your travel, if not all of it, is a tax-deductible expense.

One way you could do that is by owning a travel business. Let's say you want to travel more often. You can develop a strategic alliance with a travel provider and sell approximately ten seats, let's say, on a cruise, and then you will receive one free. Many families do this as a way of being able to go on the cruise. Once you've sold enough to take yourself or your family, the rest will be profits paid as commissions. By doing so, you've clearly shown intent to make a profit.

Another way to travel is to take business trips where you have a purpose for traveling and doing business, versus merely taking a vacation. It's a different way of looking at the same thing, but one way keeps money in your pocket.

The IRS says that if you have a legitimate business-related purpose for traveling and if you work more than four hours and one minute that day, your travel expenses there and back are 100 percent deductible. Your meals and entertainment are 50 percent deductible, and your hotel room is 100 percent deductible.

You must keep accurate records documenting the purpose of the meetings, activities, or whatever purpose you choose. What you do with the other twenty hours of time there is up to you. That's where the fun comes in! If you take the next five days off and don't work at all, the travel expense there and back is still 100 percent deductible. You receive the meal/entertainment and hotel deduction for the days you have a legitimate business-related purpose for having traveled there.

What is a legitimate purpose for being there? I can think of all sorts of meetings and research I must complete and need to travel for. For example, if you were in the travel business, you would view the beaches, eat at the local restaurants, visit hotels, and speak with travel-service providers to make good recommendations to clients, wouldn't you?

Get Real!

Look great, feel great, and live a long time as part of your business

I hope you're getting the idea that you can take something that's important to you, such as traveling, spending time with your loved ones, or staying as healthy as possible, and turn it into a small business. It makes complete sense to turn what you want and what you love to do into a business enterprise so that you can do more of it!

Just like being into motorcycles or travel, you can also promote healthy-living products and services if healthy living is important to you. It certainly is to me. In effect, what you are doing is customizing your small business for the life you want to live.

Get Real!

Treat your career like a business, whether or not you are working for someone else

In the long run, we're really already working for ourselves even if we work for someone else. Nobody stays in one place anymore. People move from company to company and have no more loyalty to a company than the company has to them. People are smart and value themselves more than the good of the company.

Whether you are an employee or self-employed, your career needs to be thought through, well planned, and executed. I want you to see yourself as your own business with marketable skills, talents, ideas, and time for sale. Charge a premium for your services, because if you don't, either your employer or your competitor will.

Generally, employers pay just enough so people won't quit, and some people work just hard enough so they don't get fired. Position yourself for the highest and best return of your time invested. Put yourself first. Take care of Number One.

Get Real!
Act now, because options are closing fast

The options are closing fast. Fewer and fewer good jobs are becoming available. The chasm is quickly opening. Lower-paying jobs are replacing higher-paying ones. The good ones are quickly either being replaced by technologies, shipped overseas, or being outsourced. This pattern is not going to reverse itself at any time in your lifetime. We are moving forward at a fast pace into a society of highly efficient small business operators. The day and age of an industrial, manufacturing-based economy is gone, and you are welcome to move to China and work for $3 a day if you want to.

Employers are in the business of making shareholders happy, making the executive officers wealthy, and maintaining the status quo as best they can. They need a ship that's steady, with low labor costs. They must remain extremely competitive in a growing global economy where competitors are manufacturing for 50 percent or less cost than they used to, by going overseas to do it.

Employers have limits on what they can give a workforce. They must limit wages, benefits, and retirement contributions, and they must demand results. From their point of view, they do everything they can to treat their workforce fairly. In most cases, they don't have anything left. That's why you see brilliant companies such as Service Merchandise fall off the face of the Earth. That's why Kmart can hardly stay afloat; that's why IBM almost went out of business in the early nineties. Even the best of the best can't always make it work. They want to. They try their best—but the best they have to offer, in many cases, isn't good enough anymore.

Get Real!

Your career isn't a dress rehearsal; you have only one time around

You must maximize your time by investing it in growing a small business on a part-time basis. Invest the money, time, and effort to grow your business into something you can enjoy. Create a salable equity that creates financial safety and security.

It's a new day in America. It's the rise of American free enterprise, and it's time to act so you won't be caught in the deep, deep chasm between those who have and those who don't. The question remains: Do you really have an option not to? I don't believe you do. It's getting late, and you don't want to miss this wave. Now you know that owning and operating a personal enterprise is absolutely a must-have part of your *Get Real! Game Plan for 21st Century Success.*

The next step is learning how to operate successfully for maximum success.

CHAPTER 13

How to Be Assured Success in Any Business—Beginner to Advanced

YOU CAN PROTECT YOURSELF and be assured of success in business once you understand the power of the "80/20 Rule." This rule applies to brand new business owners as well as seasoned veterans.

Get Real!
The 80/20 Rule

Here are some examples of the 80/20 Rule:

- Eighty percent of what we eat gives us 20 percent of our nutrition.

- Only 20 percent of our nutrition comes from 80 percent of what we eat.

- Eighty percent of all money is earned by 20 percent of the population.

- Only 20 percent of the population earns 80 percent of the money.

- Eighty percent of our time is spent on accomplishing only 20 percent of our results.

- Twenty percent of what we achieve takes up 80 percent of our time.

The 80/20 Rule extends to everything we do. Begin to notice this important principle at work. Ask yourself where and how the 80/20 Rule can be leveraged to your advantage in business.

For example, when I make my daily action plan, I plan everything I do by following the 80/20 Rule. I ask myself which important task is a 20 percent item that gives me 80 percent of the results I want. Then I schedule to accomplish as many 20 percent items as possible first to get 80 percent of my most important work done. I may not even get to the 80 percent items. And if not, nothing significant is lost.

Let's assume financial security is high on your list of financial priorities. You've identified it as a high-priority 20 percent item that gives you 80 percent of what you want related to finances. Define which activities must be done to accomplish this goal. That's applying the 80/20 Rule to your financial situation.

The strategies you are about to learn are the top 20 percent strategies that will give you 80 percent of true business success. Master them and business success is guaranteed.

Get Real!

Learn the business process of interacting with a potential customer/client, developing a relationship, forming a trust—then serving the client

Think for a minute about what business really is. Good business is a simple process that works like this:

1. Communicating with potential customer/clients
2. Converting a prospect into a customer/client
3. Developing a relationship by serving them well
4. Establishing trust over time
5. Continuing to provide other products and services that the client wants

The secret is in *serving* people and doing it well. Too many people think all that you need to do is have a good idea, product, or service; open the door; and people will come—not so. Ask anyone who's been in business. Some think that if you give a good price and good service, people will just keep on coming—not so. Business starts and ends by serving the customer/client by *giving that person what he or she wants*. No customer, no business—no money.

Before I show you the master secrets for business success, let's make sure you understand what five elements go into building a solid business plan.

The Business Plan	
1. Description	20%
2. Marketing Plan	20%
3. Competition	20%
4. Management/Employees	20%
5. Financial	20%
	100%

Put the 80/20 Rule to work here. Which part of the business plan do you think is the 20 percent activity that produces 80 percent of real results in business?

Get Real!
Apply the 80/20 Rule for your business success

That's right—marketing. Marketing is the master secret for success in any business, and that's what the majority of business owners in America don't know. You may be getting by without knowing much about marketing, but don't expect to bank your financial future on luck. Business has little to do with luck and a lot to do with good marketing strategy. It's time for you to *become the expert at marketing your business.* If you're just starting in business, you've got to be the one in charge, not the advertising salespeople. You'll want to have an excellent handle on this part of your business. I want you to be the expert at marketing your business rather than the technician who works in the business.

Get Real!
Work on your business, not in your business

By the end of this chapter, you will have learned the key ingredients for successful marketing strategy, what to do, and how to do it. I had one business I ran for ten years of blood, sweat, and tears. I didn't understand strategic marketing other than to accept and do what the advertising salespeople suggested I do. I was spending money on advertising not knowing what I would get out of it. It was a lot of hoping and praying.

Here's what you hear from advertising salespeople: "The more you do it, the better it gets." Those of us in business have heard it a thousand times. That's a recipe for disaster and a great way to go broke. It's a broken business model that makes absolutely no sense in today's world of business. Traditional approaches for reaching potential customers using old ideas are expensive, not measurable; take too long to test; and are like taking $100 bills and lighting them on fire to see if anyone notices. I'll show you how to advertise using little money, and how to measure the exact cost of acquiring a new customer, as well as the lifetime value of a new customer. The average business owner can learn some of this by doing, but that's the expensive way, will take years to figure out, and is called the school of hard knocks. You'll definitely need specialized education to understand these concepts I'm about to show you.

Get Real!

Break through unproductive preconceptions and attitudes about the marketing of products and services

Before you begin, though, you must break through any preconceptions and attitudes you have regarding marketing your products or services. Many people, including business owners, have an attitude about the idea of *selling*, as if it's a sin, or a bad thing to do. At one time, I did, too. I didn't understand that the distribution of products and services is an honorable activity. Yes, there are unscrupulous people selling products and services that are either not a good value or not professionally backed up, but that's exactly where we can make a difference. Knowing you're playing the game with integrity, honesty, and a strategy of service puts you in front of those who don't know it. Remember, *professional* selling is the highest-paid profession in the world. The key is in seeing yourself as a *professional marketer* and developing *professional* skills.

Get Real!

Become a professional and expert marketer

You won't be successful running any business if you aren't fully engaged in the process of identifying, communicating (reaching), and converting a prospect into a customer. You will starve. I want you to become a professional and expert marketer. That's what the successful business person does, and that's how they get paid. They won't get paid much by hoping and dreaming that if they build it, someone will come. It's your job to know, understand, and serve the customer better than the competition. Your potential customer has many choices of where to go for your product or service, and you've got to shine and be the one who gets through the clutter of marketing messages your potential customer sees and hears every day.

Get Real!
You're already a better marketer than you may realize

We've grown up in a continuously interrupted world full of advertising ever since we were kids. As a society, we've become *immune* to advertising messages to the point where we don't even notice them. Believe it or not, you're more of an expert in the field of marketing than you realize, having grown up with so much of it. It's time to begin to pay better attention and use much of what you already understand about marketing. Interestingly, the traditional advertising methods we grew up with have become less and less effective. It's just plain hard to reach people, catch their attention, and get them to respond. In fact, we've developed technologies to eliminate advertisements, such as the TV remote and the radio scan button. Note that TV, radio, magazines, and even the Internet to a large degree wouldn't exist if it weren't for the advertising revenue generated.

Get Real!
Know the customers/clients better than they know themselves

You must know your customers/clients better than they know themselves. Certainly you want to know the *demographics* of your customers. Demographics are such factors as age, income, family makeup, occupation, education level, and where they live. Once you know the demographic, you identify your *customer profile*. Once you know the customer profile you're after, you can begin to *target market*.

Demographics ➡ Customer Profile ➡ Target Market

These few concepts escape 90 percent of today's business owners. Most people just start a business and hope for the best by providing a product or service. The reality is: you've got to know this information to compete. Other business owners want the same customer you do. The problem is: they might know more or want the customer more than you do. In business, competing is not an option—it is the game.

Once you know your customer profile and your target market, you must look further into your customers' *buying behaviors and buying habits* to discover patterns. Modern marketers call this *psychographics*. We have developed psychographic criteria and include lifestyles, attitudes, beliefs, values, and personality. Psychographic groups are expressions of our lifestyles. Take a Chevy truck, for example. Who would be a likely buyer—a man or a woman? Definitely a man. That's not to say women don't buy Chevy trucks; we're just looking at who the most likely buyers would be. Now picture that typical Chevy truck commercial: It's a truck plowing over rocks, going up a riverbed, muddy, rugged, eager for adventure, and wild at heart. That's the little boy inside every real man, right? Now, who buys a Volvo—a man or a woman? That's right—a woman. What's the primary feature Volvo portrays in its ads? Correct—safety and security, which would appeal to women. Back to the Chevy truck—what would be the right music, a gravely voice singing "like a rock," or a romantic ballad? How about the Volvo? What about buying behaviors and buying habits? What might be another product the person driving a Chevy might be interested in buying, Bud in the can or a fine wine? How about the Volvo—Budweiser or fine wine? Would the person driving the truck and wanting a Bud be a prospect for opera tickets—or a NASCAR race? You see, you understand this because you've grown up with it. It's time to apply some of what you already understand to your business so you can profit, too.

Remember, you can build a business plan 500 pages thick, but if you can't explain to the funding agency or bank who your customers are, how they think, what they do, where they go for fun, how they spend money—you won't get the money. You must be able to talk circles around the banker when it comes to knowing the customer. You must become *the expert in knowing your customer*.

Get Real!

Continue to serve your clients by dovetailing other products or services they may want

Good business in today's world is built on *relationships*. Building a relationship with a prospective customer or client, then converting him or her into a *paying* customer or client is the key to your success. Good business is about providing excellent service and value, which establishes *trust*. Once you establish trust, you have the potential to *serve* the customer or client by providing additional products or services he or she wants and needs. This is called dovetailing or cross-selling. If you don't do it, you have inconvenienced your customers or clients, sending them on their way, forcing them to start from scratch to find someone else they can build a relationship with and learn to trust. It's all about continuing to provide products and services once you've proven that they can trust and rely on you for good value and service.

Smart business people know how to dovetail products and services to their client base. Again, by having built a relationship of trust, your clients would most prefer going to you for other products and services. That's the principle behind dovetailing. You dovetail one product or service into another that they also may want. If you don't offer it to them, they must find someone else to get it from, which is a loss for you. Besides, by forcing them to go other places you risk losing your hard-earned customers by sending them to a competitor. You must remain aware of what the customer wants. People want convenience, not a new way to spend time they don't have. I can't tell you how many times I've been in a business and when I asked for a product or service, they basically have told me, no, I can't help you, go someplace else. It hurts me to see business people throw money out the door by being unaware and shortsighted.

Get Real!

Give them what they want—not what you think they need

Always give your customers or clients what they want—which may not be what they need. For example, when we go to McDonald's are we going there to be nourished or to conveniently fill our bellies and get the kids a "Happy Meal"? That's right, we're going there because the fast-food restaurant gives us what we want, not what we need. We want convenience, a break today, and for kids to be happy for three minutes and twelve seconds—which is well worth $2.50!

Think for a minute about what bottled soda really is. It's dark sugar water, proven to add toxins to our bodies, which may cause cancer, may eventually cause adult onset diabetes, allegedly can rust off cars, and, on top of it all, is laced with caffeine to keep us pumped up! What do you think—is that what the advertisement says? Of course not. Picture the set for filming a bottled soda commercial and think about the implied benefits: The models are all younger than twenty-one (if you drink this soda, you'll have no body fat and be young forever), everyone is in prime physical health (you, too, can be beautiful and attractive), it's an incredibly sunny day (you'll feel great and won't have any worries), nobody is working and they're playing volleyball on the beach (you'll have no responsibilities), everyone is single (no one is tied down to a spouse and children), everyone has friends who have virtually no clothes on or the latest styles in beachwear (everyone belongs to the in crowd), and they're all guzzling down the fountain of youth—bottles of sugar water! The manufacturers of these products know we want to look good, feel good, and live forever—right? They portray their product as the fountain of youth and the solution to all our problems. Wow— that's advertising! They give us what we want by showing us all the *benefits* we receive by having and using their product.

Get Real!
Know the benefits from owning or having your product or service

Your product or service is not so much about what it can do (features) as it is about what it does for the client or customer (benefits). Are you selling tax services, or providing a hedge of *protection* from the IRS, a *comfort* level knowing that a professional has prepared the forms? Are you in the haircutting business, or in the business of helping women *feel beautiful* about themselves? Are you a landscaper, or the one who can make me *feel proud* about my yard when I come home from a day's work? You must look deeper and discover exactly what benefits a potential customer or client receives by doing business with you. Remember, if you don't know the real benefits you offer, you may get outsmarted, because in the real world there's always a Wal-Mart or some similar competitor moving in close by.

Get Real!
Know your competition better than they know themselves

An important part of any marketing plan is identifying the current competition as well as potential competition. Remember, *it's your competitor's job to put you out of business*. If they're interested in growing their business, many times it will involve converting your clients to theirs. You'll want to become aware of *who* they are, the *market share* they control, and *why they're successful.* Don't kid yourself—the new player on the block can quickly become the big cheese. Look at Dell Computer, for example. Mike Dell was a college student who started assembling computers for his friends and small businesses in the early 1980s in his dorm room. Meanwhile, IBM, the big International Business Machines Company, was convinced that since it was in the "business machine business," it knew better and there would be no need for those silly little machines called PCs for people's desks.

Get Real!
Don't kid yourself—you can be outsmarted and not even know it

Big Blue continued to focus on its core business, which were mainframe computers. Meanwhile, little Michael Dell was outsmarting them. Eventually, he completely changed the way IBM, Hewlett-Packard, and most other computer manufacturers did business. Today, Dell operates a $32 billion-a-year business. He has completely changed the landscape of how computers are manufactured and delivered to the user. In fact, most leading competitors have adopted his methods of distribution just to stay alive. Please don't kid yourself—if the big dogs like HP or IBM can get outsmarted, so can you.

Get Real!
Do some investigative research and learn about and from your competitors

I suggest that you do some *competitive research* by setting up files on your competition. Start by making notes on everything you see, hear, or know about potential competitors to your business. You want to have an upper hand by knowing them well, maybe even better than they know themselves. Let's say you want to open a restaurant. What do you think would be a smart way to investigate the competition before you actually open your doors? That's right—visit the competition, eat there, study the menu, watch the customers come in and out, ask servers questions like "What are the top 20 percent items everybody always orders around here?" Find out who the owner is, befriend him or her, and ask questions like: "Mrs. Smith, you have a beautiful restaurant. How long have you been in the business? What is the secret to your success?" You'll be surprised what you'll learn if you're willing to ask. They don't need to know you're considering opening a restaurant down the road. They'll be pleased you took an interest in their masterpiece.

Get Real!
Develop your own Unique Selling Proposition

Another little-known secret for business success is creating a USP. The USP stands for *unique selling proposition* or *unique selling position*. Tom Monihan, the man who started Domino's Pizza, was just a college student who was hungry one day, didn't have a car, and wanted some pizza. Back in his day, no one delivered pizza. He went on to change the way America eats pizza by launching a delivery service that eventually became Domino's and has made him millions of dollars. He has gone on to support charitable work around the world and has given away millions to the less fortunate, all because he knew his USP. You, too, must define what sets you apart from the rest, or you'll look like just another one of them.

USPs need to be fluid, because competition may pick up on yours and use it themselves. Who invented the "Kid's Meal"? McDonald's . . . maybe? But doesn't every other fast-food place now have a "Kid's Meal"? To remain unique, you must remain awake and ready to make changes utilizing new USPs.

Get Real!
Begin marketing efforts by using the end-in-mind strategy

A successful marketing plan begins with the end in mind. Consider the story of a couple who attended one of my *Get Real! Money Seminars*. They had been professional clergy for forty years and were now retired and wanted to open a small business to have a supplementary income for retirement. They had about $115,000 to invest in a small business. She happened to be an outstanding artist, so they decided to make lithographs of several of her paintings. They printed an inventory costing around $100,000. Then they followed the advice of an advertising salesperson who suggested that the way to sell the prints was to take a full-page, four-color ad in a national magazine, costing the entire $15,000 they had left. Guess what happened? They were left with $100,000 of inventory.

That was a huge setback for these new entrepreneurs, considering that it was their life savings and that they needed the money to produce ongoing income, not suck them dry. Compare that to an entrepreneur I once heard speak who launched a multimillion-dollar business knowing that Americans want to *look good, feel good, and live forever*. He decided to test his idea by taking out an inexpensive ad in *USA Today* that read something like this: "Look good, feel good, and extend your life—800-555-5555."

He said he got such a huge response that he calculated he could have taken approximately $50,000 in orders. He then decided, "Maybe I should find something to sell these people!" He went on to launch a nutritional supplement company. He was thinking and acting like an entrepreneur by starting with the end in mind first, then *testing the idea—even before he had invested in inventory or infrastructure*. This happens all the time with small business owners. They think they have a great idea, set up shop, and don't have a clue about whether or not people really want what they have to offer—or if they can cost-effectively reach people to build a profitable long-term relationship.

Get Real!
Discover the most efficient method of communicating with your target market

Every business needs to discover the *most efficient method* of communicating with its target market. I can't tell you what is best for you without getting to know you and your business personally. You must find the best marketing method for you, because your business will depend upon it. Let me give you an example of what I mean. The best medium for a plumber would be a Yellow Pages listing. Notice I didn't say a Yellow Pages ad; I said a listing. Very important, though, is the name the plumber uses for the business.

Notice that "Zebra Plumbing" is no longer in business in your area! A good name would be something like *AAAAAAAAAA Fast, Easy to Deal With, I'll Be Right There, Good Guy Plumber*. When people need a plumber, they don't look on the Internet, watch for a TV ad, or look in a magazine—they go to the Yellow Pages and go down the alphabetical list, clear and simple. If you're first on the list, you have a good chance of getting a call. Unfortunately, it's not that simple for most businesses, and you must *test* for which vehicle is best for you. Here's a list of traditional advertising methods that I call "hit-or-miss marketing":

1. Yellow Pages

2. Print Ads

3. Radio

4. TV

5. Direct Mail

6. Billboards

Get Real!

Stay away from hit-or-miss advertising methods unless you are absolutely sure they are worth the money

I recommend staying away from all six of theses hit-or-miss forms of advertising for now unless you are sure your business will profit from them. You'll go broke if you're not sure of what you are doing. You don't have the money to build brand awareness, cut through advertising clutter, and build a business using traditional advertising—there is a much better way. You need to be more sophisticated and strategic in your approach. Let everybody else do it by hit-and-miss.

Get Real!

Get Real! Marketing Strategy™

Remember, your financial future depends on your ability to reach people, build a relationship based on trust, and secure a long-term customer or client. You must identify as quickly as possible what is the most efficient method of reaching them.

Get Real! Marketing Strategy uses state-of-the-art marketing methods that consist of four primary marketing tactics. Visit www.GetRealMoney.com under Small Business for more details about *Get Real! Marketing Strategy* as well as a FREE training telephone conference on the subject. I'll walk you through each of them, showing you how to use each strategy starting right away, costing you little to nothing.

Get Real! Marketing Strategy

1. **Direct Response Marketing**
   Where results can be measured.

2. **Database Marketing**
   Collection of targeted names, addresses, numbers, or e-mail addresses that can be used to communicate.

3. **Referral Marketing**
   Word of mouth/networking.

4. **Permission Marketing**
   When a person gives you permission to periodically contact him or her.

Get Real!

Develop copywriting skills

One skill that is especially important in all the marketing strategies, but especially Direct Response Marketing, is copywriting. Copywriting is the skill of persuasively using words to capture attention. Your goal is to capture readers' attention long enough to get them to respond to your message. We know that certain words carry weight in the mind of the consumer. Good copywriting is the tool for conveying the benefits your product or service offers to people. Having a good working knowledge of which words to use and how and when to use them will make a huge difference in your response rates when advertising.

For example, suppose you want to place a classified ad in the local paper for your business. A well-written classified ad has three parts: the *grabber headline*, the *copy*, and the *offer.* The grabber headline is the first and only thing you want people to read. If your headline is effective, they will read the *copy*, and if the body copy is effective, they'll respond to your direct-response *offer.* Below are a few examples. Tell me which you would respond to if you were looking for a house.

> **FOR SALE: $89,000, good house, good schools, close to pool, call 555-5555.**

> **FREE MONEY! Buy my house and I'll give you $5,000 at closing, 24 hr. recorded message for details, call 555-5555.**

At this point in the marketing process, my goal is not to sell the house. It's to get potential buyers to call and listen to the recorded message, which is where I'll give the details of what I am offering as well as a way to leave their name and number. That way, I'm not answering a phone and giving people useless information they may or may not really want. I'm using good copywriting and a strategic *qualifying process* combined with a *direct response* strategy. (P.S.—can I sell the house for $94,000 and give them $5,000 at closing and still get the same price for the house?)

Get Real!
Know the lifetime value of your customer or client

Once you know how to best reach your target market, the next step is to calculate the *lifetime value* of your customer or client. Here's a simple equation. Once you understand, you'll never look at business the same way again:

<$10.00>	**Advertising/conversion cost** *Cost to convert target market prospect into customer or client*
<$14.18>	**Expense for doing business first time** *Expense providing new customer with a product or service*
<$24.18>	**Total expense for acquiring new customer**
$978.23	**Average income generated over lifetime** *3.2 years average life of new customer*
<$542.33>	**Average cost of doing business, including initial loss of $24.18**
$435.90	**Average net profit for each newly acquired customer**

The question comes down to this: how many times would you trade $24.18 to make $435.90 over a 3.2-year period? What you've done is reduce the entire process of doing business to a simple mathematical equation. You can do this because you can calculate the real costs of acquiring a new customer or client, as well as know how long that person remains a client and how much you can make over that defined period of time.

Get Real!
Test, test, test

I mentioned a principle earlier that I want to make sure you remember. I used the word *test*. *Get Real! Marketing Strategy* is about test after test after test. You test the mailer, the headline, the words spoken on the phone, the color of the direct-mail piece. All these variables are important, and they all must be tested at some point in your process of forming a marketing strategy. By the way, you never really arrive. There are so many variables that you can't test everything.

Suppose you send three direct-mail pieces—one timed to arrive on Thursday, another one on Friday, and another on Saturday. You want to find out which day would give you the best response rate. Great, that's one test. But suppose the batch for Thursday gets lost in the mail and arrives a day later than expected. Maybe it was sunny on the Friday the mailer came and the next time you tried it was cloudy. *Everything matters.* What you try to do is *test for aspects you can control,* such as the day, the color, the headline, or the offer. Your job is to keep good records, as if you were conducting a scientific experiment. Once you find success, you then repeat it often.

You *can* become a master at marketing, too. Become a student of the process, remembering this is the 20 percent aspect of business that will give you 80 percent of your overall success in business. Marketing will either make you or break you. You may have the greatest products or services in the world, but if you can't market them effectively, you're stuck holding the bag. Commit to the process by developing a success library; get specific training and remember the 80/20 Rule. Eighty percent of your success in business is a result of powerful marketing.

Next I'll show you where the money is going to come from to run your business and how to get your hands on it.

CHAPTER 14

How to Get Real! Money for Business

TO LAUNCH, GROW, OR RUN A BUSINESS TAKES MONEY. It may not take as much as you think, and it may not have to be yours. In this chapter I'll show you the best strategies for starting, operating, and growing a small business—on a shoestring. I've used these strategies to do just that.

Get Real!
Start with a business plan

Before you can ask someone to fund your business idea or expansion, you must have a written plan. Everybody you talk to has a great business idea— but the money goes to the person who has it *written down*. Remember the five parts of a business plan—description, marketing plan, competition, management/employees, and financial? They are all important, but as I said, the marketing plan is the most important. Putting other people's money to work on your idea is more about knowing how to create "win-win" agreements.

Get Real!
Money finds those who know exactly what they want and where they are going

Money is attracted to those who know exactly what they want, have a plan to get it done, and can show others what's in it for them. The business plan defines exactly what the money is used for, how much is needed, and when you'll need it. Once you can answer these questions, you can begin the search for money. That's when you bring your business to a new level.

Remember, a bank, government agency (as in the case of a grant, loan, or subsidy), or the seller of a business who may finance you wants to know about you, the partner. When you borrow money from anyone, the other party is looking at you and asking themselves the same questions you must be asking yourself.

Get Real!
When looking for financing from a bank, government agency, or the seller, you are asking them to be your partner

Here's what they want to know: "Am I going to get my money back with interest? Does the borrower know what he or she is doing? What is the collateral in case the borrower doesn't pay? What benefits, strengths, and assets does the borrower bring to the table? Is my neck on the line?" When it comes to getting other people to partner with you in a business venture, it's nuts-and-bolts time. They're investing in your idea and becoming your business partner by supplying financing.

You must show your potential partner what you bring to the table—a viable business idea, ingenuity, sweat equity, creativity, and courage. Besides that, you might have to bring personal assets such as personal savings, equity in property, retirement accounts, lines of credit, life insurance cash value, or the title to your car. Believe it or not, that's how more than 70 percent of businesses are started in America—personal savings and/or personal assets. I've used every one of the above in business ventures I've built over the last twenty-five years.

I'm not suggesting that you should do the same. What I am saying is that this is reality. Suppose you need $10,000, $20,000 or $100,000 to purchase equipment, supplies, build a Web site, and get support and training to move forward. Where is it going to come from? First, compare this to what most people do today to acquire a college diploma. A college education involves four to six years of effort, with expenses of at least $40,000. The whole idea is to become more employable and able to earn a better living, right? Compare that to the idea of owning and operating a business.

Ask any business owner how much he or she has invested in equipment and supplies. Even for a very small business, it will probably be well into the tens of thousands of dollars. One woman I trained started her embroidery business fourteen years ago with a $40,000 investment in equipment. She now has $220,000 invested. Another man I helped had invested well over $750,000 in equipment to operate his business. I've worked closely with thousands of business owners who have made large investments to start and continuously run their businesses. I've worked with many others who have invested less than $1,000 and are earning substantial incomes. The initial investment doesn't necessarily equal a better business or a better rate of return on money invested. That's why you must look closely at the rate of return for any business venture.

Get Real!

Tap into any and all government grants, loans, or subsidies available

An excellent source of money for business is the federal

government. Today more than ever, the government is making grants, loans, and subsidies available for small business. Our government knows that small businesses with twenty-five or fewer employees create 75 percent of all new jobs in America. The government also knows that it gets paid before the worker gets paid, through a payroll deduction. It works well for the government to support the creation of jobs in America. Our government is interested in supporting small business like never before. The government agency called the Small Business Administration has two excellent programs worth looking into for the small business owner:

Microloan: The Microloan provides both start-up and/or operating capital for a small business, and is available for up to $25,000.

LowDoc Loan: The Low Documentation loan is also for start-up and/or operating capital, but is available for up to $150,000. The LowDoc loan application is designed for a quick approval turnaround time.

The government also has money available through the U.S. Department of Agriculture (USDA). This money is specifically used for funding rural-area businesses. A rural area is typically qualified as being a town population of 20,000 or less. For those willing to do the research and submit grant request proposals, this is well worth the effort.

Get Real!

Seller financing is a powerful resource for starting or growing a business

One area of getting money for business that's overlooked, because most people just do not know to ask, is seller financing. Sellers will often finance the sale of a business or business assets to help sell the business. When an owner decides it's time to move on, he or she doesn't put a "For Sale" sign in the front yard. It's not like real estate, which you expect people to sell from time to time. Many sellers get into problems and are forced to sell because of poor health, divorce, or death in the family. Many times the owner will become highly motivated to sell, but doesn't know how to sell the business easily. Remember, banks do not like to lend money on used businesses where the seller is leaving. In many cases, business owners are forced to owner finance as well as selling at a considerable discount.

This creates a huge opportunity for those in the hunt. I had a student act on an assignment I gave at one *Get Real! Money Seminar*. He needed another rig for his trucking business. I suggested he make a few phone calls to competitors and ask if any of them had equipment for sale and might be motivated. He came back the next morning with a bill of sale for a new trailer he needed. He was excited because he negotiated a zero-down purchase, zero percent interest at 50 cents on the wholesale dollar, and free and clear title! That's a whole lot better than going to a bank, jumping through hoops, waiting for weeks, and missing a great opportunity.

Get Real!
Go into business without having to start one

Seller financing is a great way to get into a business without having to start one. Many existing business owners would love to sell their businesses if they only had someone they felt they could trust who would buy it, operate it well, and make a monthly payment in a timely and responsible manner. I always recommend that if a person is going to start a business from scratch, he or she should first look into purchasing an existing business from a motivated seller willing to finance. You can negotiate for the existing owner to be an on-call consultant for several years in case you need expertise along the way.

When the seller finances the sale of the business, he or she becomes the bank and takes back what is known as a note. A note is an IOU, which states how much you owe, how it will be paid back, when it will be paid, and what happens if you don't. Typically there will be a Uniform Commercial Code (UCC) filing at the local courthouse, putting the public on notice that there is a lien on equipment and/or the business assets. It works much like a trust deed or a mortgage on real estate.

Get Real!

When negotiating for seller financing, prepare to win on either price or terms

When you structure a seller-financed deal, you must negotiate a win-win agreement. The problem is, what "win" means to one person may not be a "win" to another. Typically, in a seller-financed situation, the seller wants his *price* in a negotiation. That's fine, as long as you get your *terms*. It's one or the other, and you typically don't get both and neither will the seller. The *terms* are the *length of years* to pay back the loan, the *interest rate*, and the amount of the *payment*.

Get Real!

Find out what is most important to the seller by first asking good questions and listening well

When you are negotiating for the seller to finance the sale of his or her business, you'll need some ammunition to make it attractive to that person. You've got to put yourself in the seller's shoes by asking yourself: What would I want out of this if I were him or her? That's smart thinking as a negotiator; always determine what the other party wants first. It's easy to know what you may want, and not so easy to determine what they want. The best way to learn what a seller wants is by asking good open-ended questions and listening well. Here are excellent questions to ask to get an idea of exactly what's important to the seller in this situation.

- ■ What would you like to get out of this transaction?
- ■ How much money do you need right away, and for what purpose?
- ■ Do you have something in mind that you were planning on using the money for?
- ■ What type of investment would you make if you had this lump sum of money now?

Once you have a better idea of what the seller needs or wants, you can structure your offer to try to best meet those needs. Suppose the seller expresses a desire to retire, stop working, and take time to travel in an RV. He's just given you the answer to what to present to him. What does a retiree need or want—a lump sum of cash he must pay capital gains tax on, then reinvest and manage? Or, how about a monthly check for the rest of his life, capital gains tax deferred, his money invested at a decent rate of return and backed up by the business assets he wants sold?

Get Real!
The Loan Schedule Strategy™

At this point, instead of asking the seller to finance the sale, you present an offer using *The Loan Schedule Strategy* and show him what's in it for him. Print out an amortization schedule of the proposed loan you'll be negotiating for, tape it together vertically top to bottom, and then highlight the entire interest earned column. Then present your offer, using the script below:

I have a way to help us both. In fact, you'll sell your business right away and start traveling.

Have you noticed how the banks own the nicest buildings in town? You'll have the opportunity to be the bank.

You will also defer your capital gains tax.

Your money will remain invested and receive an attractive rate of return.

You'll receive a nice monthly income from me, which will be deposited into your bank and can be used for gas money or whatever you want for the next ten years. (Stand on a chair, let the loan schedule fall to the floor. It's usually five to ten pages long. Show it to the seller.)

Which would you rather me do, give all this money to the bank, or should I send it all to you instead?

You just showed the seller what's in it for him! This powerful strategy gets results, and can be used for negotiating real estate seller financing as well.

The Loan Schedule Strategy

1. Seller gets to be the bank
2. Seller defers capital gains tax
3. Seller keeps his or her money invested
4. Seller receives monthly cash flow

Get Real!

Create separate notes and liens when purchasing real estate and business assets

One important aspect of a business sale transaction is to be sure to separate business assets and real estate by making them two separate transactions rather than one and the same. It works better for both parties this way. Having been involved with purchasing business notes and real estate notes from owners who have them, I know that business notes have a significantly different market value than does a real estate note. See www.GetRealMoney.com under Real Estate.

Get Real!

Negotiate the purchase of the business based on future performance, giving the seller a portion of the earnings

Another strategy for financing the purchase or sale of a business is an agreement based on profits or performance. A buyer may not be sure the claimed track record is absolutely correct. The best way to substantiate a business' performance is to request tax returns that verify what the seller claimed as income—not what the seller says you can make. Always purchase a business based on real numbers, not under-the-table business. If the sellers have run the business without claiming all the income, it will be to their detriment when they sell the business. Unclaimed income will convert to a smaller market value of the business when it comes time to sell.

In this case, a seller can agree to receive a portion of the gross of net revenue generated. Another important aspect of a business sale is to be sure to include a non-compete agreement so the seller can't just open up a new shop down the road. The seller agrees not to compete for a period of time and/or within a specific geographic area. See www.GetRealMoney.com under Small Business for information on buying or selling an existing business.

Get Real!

For larger business financing deals, consider "angel" investors

Private investment groups, called "angel" investors, fund certain types of business ventures. They are interested in making investments, mostly in start-up companies. Once they do, they expect to hire operating officers as well as take majority share ownership.

Get Real!
The Strategic Alliance Strategy™

The *Strategic Alliance Strategy* is a powerful method of growing a business, limiting your liabilities, remaining flexible, and staying competitive. One of your goals will be to remain flexible with as little liability exposure as possible. One of the best ways to do this is to delegate and contract work to strategic alliances, keeping you ready to respond quickly to changes in the marketplace. One example of a strategic alliance could work like this: You operate a business distributing products that a well-respected company manufactures, packages, and ships to an end user; bills the customer for you; handles customer relations; and pays you a commission without your ever handling the product.

Another example of a strategic alliance would be your team of hired experts. Your team may include an attorney, a CPA, a real estate agent, a handyman/contractor, a title company, an insurance agent, etc. These all become your alliances of specialists so you don't have to know it all. The same is true for service providers. You can hire the local Kinko's for your printing needs and not even own a copy machine. You can use a UPS Store as your shipping and receiving department. You can even lease employees! The secret is in knowing how to streamline operations, contract out as much as possible, and not lose control.

Get Real!
Before you start a business or grow a business to a new level, ask the right questions

As I train business owners, I always ask them to answer several questions *before* they launch or expand a business.

■ **Do I want to start or grow my business, or do I want to make twice as much money—in half the time?**

What answer do you think I get ninety-nine out of one hundred times? In most cases, growing a business will result in more employees, more work to do, and more liability issues. That's why I stress the *Business Blueprint* and the idea of building a life—not merely a business. It's way too easy to get off track from what we really want.

Knowing and deciding what you want *ahead of time* is 80 percent of the battle. Apply the 80/20 Rule when answering these questions for yourself as you move forward.

■ **Where do 80 percent of my profits come from in my current business? What activities do I receive 80 percent of my satisfaction from doing?**

If you don't answer these questions before you move forward, *you'll end up with a business—but not a life.* Knowing what segment of your business makes 80 percent of the real money is essential. Once you determine this, do a lot more of it and you'll end up making more money. Spend less effort working on the portion of your business that produces only 20 percent of the profits. You'll free up more time to work *on* your business rather than *in* it.

Most business people have certain activities they just love to do and activities they hate to do. Play to your strengths. Delegate details you don't enjoy and invest more time doing what you do enjoy. Business should be fun, invigorating, and fulfilling—not a chore.

Get Real!
Bigger isn't always better

Many seasoned owners have grown their businesses only to find that they have less time for living and don't end up enjoying their business as much as they used to. Even though they've grown their business bigger, it's not more profitable. There is a point at the peak of the bell curve where you maximize the potential of the business. That's why having the ability to operate business like an entrepreneur, using proven principles you can imprint on any business, will help you. Maybe operating an entirely new business or starting a new division may be the route to go, instead of expanding what you already have. I've heard many owners say, "It was great in the good old days—just me, myself, and I." Bigger isn't always better.

Get Real!
Do it now!

You are now equipped with the strategies and principles that will make you successful part-time or full-time in business. There's only one more thing left to do—decide to move forward. Take the next step. For those of you who are new, decide what your *Business Blueprint* is going to be by taking the time to design one. Look at options, set a deadline, and get running. For those of you who are seasoned—same thing. Redesign your *Business Blueprint*, look at your options, and move forward. You'll be glad you did.

Having an additional income stream working for you is a great feeling. Having several income streams working for you feels even better. Now let me show you the most proven method for providing you and your family with permanent financial security.

CHAPTER 15

Get Real! Money Security: Real Estate Strategy

MASTER SECRET #5 IS *REAL ESTATE STRATEGY*. Real estate is clearly the most proven method as well as the most conservative method of developing a secure financial future. More people have developed permanent financial security through real estate than in any other way. Real estate is one of the safest investments, if done intelligently, and is one of the only investments and businesses in which you can start with nothing and turn it into thousands of dollars in a relatively short period of time. Your rate of investment return can be well over 300 percent in many cases. This is a phenomenal strategy for developing your own permanent financial security, and should be taught to everyone before they leave high school. Real estate must be part of your *Get Real! Game Plan for 21st Century Success.*

Get Real!

Real estate is the IDEAL investment for five dynamic reasons:

1. **Income:** You can generate a recurring income stream called cash flow from rental property. Someone else is paying the mortgage, taxes, upkeep, etc. That's the magic—you own it; they pay for it. The income from a piece of real estate goes up consistently with time. The same house your parents rented years ago for $100 a month would now rent for more than $700. It's the same house, just forty years older, more worn down, and the *rent keeps increasing*.

2. **Depreciation:** The government provides a *special tax benefit* for owning real estate. Over a period of years you can depreciate the real property (fair market value less the land value, which cannot be depreciated) and in turn provide a tax deduction and create a tax break. This deduction creates more money in your pocket, not Uncle Sam's.

3. **Equity:** As the property appreciates in value and the mortgage is paid down, this creates equity. Equity is the difference between what a property is worth and what is owed against it.

4. **Appreciation:** Real estate throughout the United States has appreciated (risen in value) on average 3 percent annually over the last one hundred years. Study the chart on the next page and think about the impact of being able to protect the value of money through real estate.

5. **Leverage:** Real estate is one of the best investments you'll ever make, because there are so many people willing to be your financial partner. The most conservative lenders in America will be your 70 percent financial partners at current interest rates. You can't do that with a typical business, but you can do it all day long in real estate.

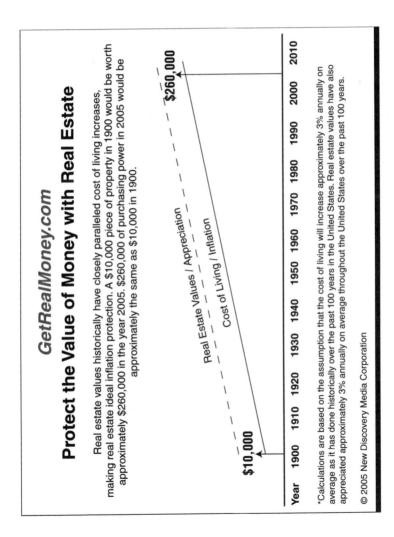

GetRealMoney.com

Protect the Value of Money with Real Estate

Real estate values historically have closely paralleled cost of living increases, making real estate ideal inflation protection. A $10,000 piece of property in 1900 would be worth approximately $260,000 in the year 2005. $260,000 of purchasing power in 2005 would be approximately the same as $10,000 in 1900.

$260,000

$10,000

Real Estate Values / Appreciation

Cost of Living / Inflation

Year 1900 1910 1920 1930 1940 1950 1960 1970 1980 1990 2000 2010

*Calculations are based on the assumption that the cost of living will increase approximately 3% annually on average as it has done historically over the past 100 years in the United States. Real estate values have also appreciated approximately 3% annually on average throughout the United States over the past 100 years.

© 2005 New Discovery Media Corporation

Get Real!
Make real estate a part of your overall wealth-building plan

Real estate needs to be an integral part of any person's wealth-building plan. Whether you own one home in your lifetime or you run a business, you will need a place to live in or operate out of. If you don't own it, you'll be paying someone else for the privilege. I suggest you make sure you are the owner rather than letting somebody else make all the money.

Real estate has a long history of creating wealth, not only in America but around the world. Real estate has maintained value on par with the Consumer Price Index (CPI), which is a calculation of the cost of goods and services. The CPI has increased steadily by approximately 3 percent per year over the last one hundred years in America. That's why real estate is an excellent inflation protection mechanism. Think about the average person, who, from the age he or she leaves home, will need a place to live for the next fifty to seventy years. People don't have to own a car, but everyone needs a place to rest his or her head.

I purchased my first home when I was twenty-one years old. I was sick and tired of paying someone else rent. When I was eighteen, I was renting an old farmhouse with my friend Dave for $200 a month. Dave asked if I'd like to jointly buy the house. I declined, thinking it was too big a commitment and really not believing it was possible. Dave went ahead anyway with the arrangements to buy the property. With just a small deposit, several weeks later he was the owner of the farmhouse and my landlord. Remember, Dave was eighteen, too! I was surprised and a little envious, yet I was happy, because now my lease was more secure—or at least I thought so.

One sunny day a mutual friend of ours named Mitch arrived with a huge couch. He and a buddy wedged the couch through the door and plopped it down in the living room. I asked what was going on. He told me that Dave had agreed to rent Mitch the living room as his new "home"—without even asking me what I thought! I guess Dave realized I would not be crazy about the idea. Still, I gave the situation a chance. Mitch was a great guy, and as bachelor living goes, I figured it would be fun having him as a roommate.

Two weeks later when the rent was due, I learned a valuable lesson about owning real estate. Remember, Dave and I previously had been renting the place from a farmer who was charging us $100 each per month. When Dave bought the place, he told me the rent would remain the same. When Mitch moved in, I assumed we would now be splitting the $200 three ways. Well, I assumed wrong. Now, I was expected to continue to pay my $100 and Mitch would pay $100, leaving Dave living there rent-free! Dave was only eighteen years old with no advanced education—but he was smart! To this day, I still thank him for being a good example and showing me it could be done if I really wanted it. It took several more years of renting before I finally took charge and decided I could be a property owner, too.

In 1979, I hardly knew what the word "credit" meant, and I didn't really understand what the prime interest rate was or that we were headed into a recession—whatever that was. I just knew that if my friend could become an investor, I could, too. I proceeded to find a property and bought it with none of my own money. Now I was the owner, rather than the tenant. That changed my life forever, and it started me investing in real estate. Learning how to invest in and buy real estate properly is absolutely a must for having more money in your life.

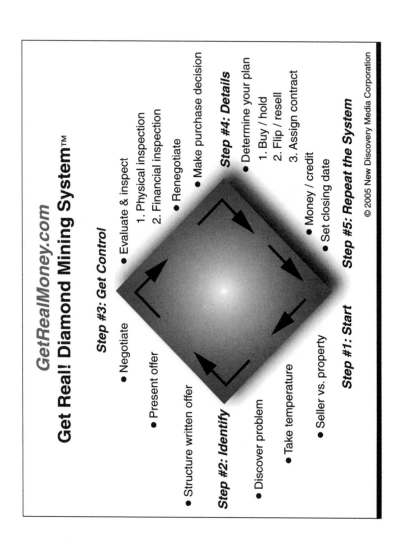

Get Real!
Use the Get Real! Diamond Mining System™ for investing in real estate

I have developed a simple and effective system for making smart real estate investments. It's called the *Get Real! Diamond Mining System* and is outlined in the chart on the next page.

Get Real! Diamond Mining System
Step #1:   Start
Step #2:   Identify
Step #3:   Get Control
Step #4:   Details
Step #5:   Repeat the System

You may be reading this and saying you just want to own a home. Well, that's exactly where I want you to start. After you purchase your home, you can make the decision to buy other property if you want to. Remember this—if you want to own your home, don't be denied, no matter what anybody says.

There will always be people to tell you what can't be done. I'm here to tell you it *will* be done if you decide to do it! But you must be the one to decide. No one can do it for you. I know home ownership can be accomplished with no money, no credit, and no job, but you must be the one to believe it. No matter what other people say, do it anyway! I have helped many people become real estate investors—and you can become one, too.

If you've already bought investment real estate, my system will create a tremendous efficiency that perhaps you've never had before. I have taught thousands of people how to invest successfully in real estate. I'm continually amazed at how many people never receive any type of education in the subject. Most people just wing it and hope for the best. Well, that may or may not be you, but I do know that the more you understand about real estate, the more profit you will earn. By knowing what you are doing, you can make more money in less time and do it with a lot less frustration.

For more details on my *Get Real! Diamond Mining System*, join us for a special telephone conference by signing up at www.GetRealMoney.com. In the conference, I'll go through each of the five steps in detail so you can begin the process for yourself. One of the most effective ways to get off to a quick start is to attend a *Get Real! Money Seminar.* I have many students who had purchase real estate *before* they attended a *Get Real! Money Seminar* and had been eaten alive for one of two reasons: either they didn't buy right or they didn't manage it well. This is one of the most common drawbacks of trying to do it entirely alone. So let's look at some tips that will help you avoid the pitfalls.

Get Real!
The Diamond Clues

Step 1 of the *Get Real! Diamond Mining System* is to locate a great deal. No, it's not in figuring out *if* you can, or *if* you have the money. It's "How do I locate an excellent opportunity and recognize it when it comes my way?" I use what is called the *Diamond Clues*™.

The Diamond Clues	
Diamond Clue #1:	Highly Motivated Seller
Diamond Clue #2:	Location
Diamond Clue #3:	Type of Property
Diamond Clue #4:	Condition
Diamond Clue #5:	Plan of Action

Diamond Clues give you a clear definition of what you are looking for. If you don't know what you are looking for, you won't know it even if it's right in front of you. By having a clearly defined *Diamond Finding Strategy*, you can recognize a diamond when it comes your way. At my *Get Real! Money Seminars*, my students consistently come back after only one day of training, having uncovered money-making deals right in their own neighborhoods.

Diamond Clue #1: Highly Motivated Seller

A motivated seller is a person who owns a piece of real estate and is anxious to sell. Most motivated sellers are looking for a solution to a major problem. I've found that most motivated sellers are usually dealing with one of four problems. You must identify the problem and then become the *problem solver*. As a person interested in improving your financial health, you must see yourself as a *professional problem solver*. Good business is about identifying problems and providing solutions for a profit.

Get Real!
Become a professional problem solver for a profit by finding motivated sellers

The four most common problems that cause sellers to become highly motivated to sell are:

1. Divorce

2. Health challenge

3. Loss of income

4. Death in the family

There may be other motivators from time to time, but generally it comes down to one of these, or a combination of several. Your goal is to discover how motivated the sellers really are—and the more motivated the better.

In your mind, imagine a thermostat that goes from zero to ten. Zero is totally uninterested in selling, no interest, they want to own the property forever. But ten is an owner whose property is going to be sold on the courthouse steps tomorrow at 10 a.m. and it's now 3 p.m. You're looking for people who are at least in the eight to ten range and must sell now because of a compelling reason. Note that you're not looking for a physical property—you're looking for a motivated seller, which is a person who typically has a problem.

Take a step back for a minute. I am not advocating that you to take advantage of a person who has hit hard times. I'm teaching you to identify a problem a person is having and offer him or her a *win-win solution.* The seller must always win for you to get what you need and want. A good offer is structured by getting in the seller's shoes, determining what he or she needs to make it work, and presenting a viable solution. Here are a few good examples:

Example 1: Mom and Dad raised three children in Lincoln, Nebraska. Daughter One moved to San Diego, the second daughter lives in Seattle, and the son is in Miami. Dad died eight years ago, and Mom just passed away this year. The family home is sitting vacant in Nebraska. Daughter One was the one who helped Mom over the years and was appointed executor of the estate. Daughter Two doesn't get along with her sister and never helped much with Mom. The son is flexible and willing to do whatever is necessary to settle the estate.

Daughter Two suddenly wants to be involved with family affairs (wants her share of the estate) and begins pressuring her sister to sell the house. The whole process is particularly painful to Daughter One, who took on most of the responsibility for helping Mom in her later years. Mom and Dad bought the house in 1964 for $9,000, and today, in its current condition, it's worth $75,000. The house needs significant updating, it's vacant, and the kids live far away. This is a common situation where you have a highly motivated seller. Daughter One has the support of her brother, wants her sister off her back, and wants the estate closed. You make a cash offer for $50,000, which is 33 percent below fair market value.

Get Real!
Create win-win solutions to problems

The executor of the estate, Daughter One, realizes that she could wait longer for more money, but decides to sell so she can move on. They take your offer, sell the house, and close the estate. They win; you win. You bought a house significantly under value. You do some basic repairs and sell it quickly under market value for a $20,000 profit. The new buyer wins by getting a good deal. That's a win, win, win!

Example 2: A seventy-four-year-old man has three investment properties he's owned for years. He's been diagnosed with cancer and can't manage them anymore. He decides it's time to get out, but he wants his asking price. He's willing to owner-finance all three to you at full price and let you send him a check every month for the next ten years. He doesn't have to deal with the property management or upkeep any more, and he looks forward to money in his checking account every month plus he gets full price. He wins. You get three great properties without going to the bank. They all have a positive cash flow meeting your investment requirements. You win.

Again, it's all about win-win—not "I win; you lose." You are a *professional* problem solver, not a person who takes advantage of people who are hurting. See yourself as helping people get what they want, and in return, you get what you want.

Get Real!
Clearly define your working area—time is money

Diamond Clue #2: Location

Define your working area or location. Get a map of the immediate local area. Indicate all the main roads and how far you can drive within ten minutes. This will be your wealth-building kingdom. It's important that you limit how far you need to drive to get to your properties, for several reasons. Time is money. You're making an investment of time when buying real estate, and you don't have time to waste, so limit the area you work based on the amount of available inventory of properties you'll need. If you live in a rural area, your drive time will be longer, because you will generally need a population base of 10,000 to have enough inventory to prime the pump of your machine. Connect the dots and promise yourself you won't go outside the cookie-cutter location. I would prefer that you become the king or queen of your smaller area, rather than the pauper of the entire county. You must draw the line somewhere, because you must focus your concentration and efforts.

Diamond Clue #3: Type of Property

What type of property do you want? Well, which car would sell faster if you had an ad in the paper—a used Honda Civic or a late-model Jaguar?

Get Real!

Keep it simple at first by investing only in residential property

That's right—basic transportation will sell faster. People need a set of wheels, not luxury. The same holds true for real estate. The most commonly sold piece of real estate is a single-family house with three bedrooms and two baths. I suggest you keep your cookie cutter clean and simple and eliminate any possible risk. You can make money in commercial property, industrial property, or raw land, but you increase the risks involved. The principle is simple—make sure the real estate provides cash flow from the get-go. For example, land may be a good investment if it has timber to cut and sell, a working oil well, productive mineral rights, or a rentable farm, but all this increases your risk. Why not just stick to residential property that can be rented from the day you buy it? Leave the other types of property for professionals who specialize in these areas. For financing purposes, residential property is considered residential when there are four or fewer units. Anything over four units will be considered commercial property in terms of packaging the financing. For now, stay away from five or more units until you have experience. Stick with residential property, four units or less. The single-family house will always sell the fastest and gives you the most flexibility.

Diamond Clue #4: Condition

The condition of the property is important, because this is where you uncover hidden value. I enjoy finding property that needs repairs. The more cosmetic repairs there are to be done, the better, in many cases. Have you ever noticed how some people will sell a car without ever having washed and waxed it? They're willing to take a huge loss just because they're too lazy to present it well. The same goes for houses. When a seller is motivated, he is typically having a financial problem and doesn't have the money to make repairs, paint rooms, fix gutters, trim landscaping, mow grass, or cut limbs. Many times he sells it in this condition, taking a loss on the real value of the property.

Get Real!

Uncover hidden values by recognizing good real estate opportunities

You'll find properties like this even in the most exclusive neighborhoods in America. You should be looking for these *tall grasses* that need basic cosmetic repairs. They are the symptom of a potentially motivated seller. I've sat in front of many houses with my cell phone, calling the tax assessor's office and asking who the owner of record is. This is public information and is available to you just by asking. My intention is to contact the owner and ask if I can *help*. Look for houses in need of repair, because these are potential gold mines.

I've asked my classes many times, "How many of you would scrub a nasty-looking tub for $500?" "Who would staple down a $20 piece of new remnant carpet in that bathroom if you could make $1,000?" I purchased a personal property from a town tax assessor at 25 percent of its actual value, because he didn't want to do these things. A little cleaning, sweeping, vacuuming, and painting can sometimes make you thousands of dollars. The assessor even loaned me the money to buy it from him and agreed not to receive payments for the first six months. By the time the first payment was due, I had already sold the property to a new buyer. These situations are not as uncommon as you might think. Every time I teach a seminar, I ask students who have purchased real estate to share one of their stories. I'm amazed at the phenomenal deals people get when they are in the hunt.

Diamond Clue #5: Plan of Action

You must have a plan. You must know what the plan is on your way in. Good real estate investing comes down to having one of two plans: Plan A and Plan B.

Get Real!

Work from a clear plan

- ■ **Plan A: Buy and Hold.** Buy and hold the property— rent it out, let the property appreciate in value, take the depreciation tax deduction, and pay off the mortgage, building equity. Your goal is to have monthly income above and beyond all operating expenses. This is called positive cash flow. I call this a *cash cow*. The opposite is called an *alligator*.

- ■ **Plan B: Quick Flip.** A quick flip is a property you intend to quickly fix up, immediately resell (in less than one year), and make a profit from. Another form of flip is assigning (selling) the contract to another investor before the closing.

At www.GetRealMoney.com, there is an entire section on Real Estate to help you determine which plan of action is best for you. Once you have your *Diamond Clues* in place, you'll know exactly what you are looking for and can use them to locate an excellent deal.

Get Real!
The Multiple Lines Strategy

You'll catch more fish with more than one line in the water. The same is true for finding great deals on real estate. Learn and use several techniques at one time. This is called the *Multiple Lines Strategy*. For example, could you have a real estate agent looking for property that fits your cookie cutter and at the same time have an ad running in the paper? While those poles are in the water, could you be paying referral fees to people who send deals your way and at the same time be driving through neighborhoods looking for "tall grasses" (poorly cared for property, indicating a potentially motivated seller)? Having a working plan for each technique is important.

Get Real!
Buy real estate wholesale

Your goal is to locate solid *wholesale* deals. Most people learn real estate through real estate agents, who are primarily in the business of helping people buy and sell their primary residences at *retail* prices. The problem is you're interested in wholesale investment property. Not every agent is dealing exclusively with retail, but few understand and know how to operate wholesale. It's important that you know how agents and brokers operate to find one who will be helpful to you. In a retail environment, you expect to negotiate 1 to 3 percent, whereas when buying wholesale, it's not uncommon to buy a property at 20 to 50 percent below fair market value.

Real estate has created more wealth than any other investment in history. President Theodore Roosevelt said it over one hundred years ago, and it is even truer today:

> "Every person who invests in well-selected real estate in a growing section of a prosperous community adopts the surest method of becoming independent, for real estate is the basis of wealth."

Now let's discuss the biggest question of all—where's the money going to come from in which to invest in real estate?

CHAPTER 16

Proven Recurring Income

IN THIS CHAPTER, YOU'LL LEARN how to operate like a professional so you attract the necessary investment money as well as saving yourself time in the process. I'm a big fan of doing whatever is necessary to work efficiently and make as much money in as little time as possible. You are about to learn strategies that even people who have been investing for years don't know. The good news is, if you are brand new to real estate, you won't spend years learning what has taken many of us years to learn. Each and every strategy here represents the nuts and bolts for the successful real estate investor.

Get Real!

Present a written offer and quickly discover how motivated the seller is

Let's suppose your agent searches the local Multiple Listings Service database and finds seven properties out of 18,000 available that fit your *Get Real!*

Diamond Mining System. What do you do? *You goal is not to spend time looking at property—it's to quickly find out how motivated a seller may be.* The best way to do that is by presenting a *written* agreement as quickly as possible—sight unseen!

The faster you get an actual offer in front of the seller, the faster you can learn how motivated the seller may or may not be. You want to weed out the sellers who are not interested in working out a deal that suits both their needs and yours. If you do this right, you get eight out of ten who say, "No thanks, not interested." That's good, because you've *sifted quickly* and didn't waste any time with a seller who isn't highly motivated. You are looking for the two out of ten who say, "Maybe." Once you've reached this point, then meet with them, inspect the properties, and put details together. When you present a real written offer, they must respond to it.

Get Real!
The Smoke 'Em Out Strategy™

Developing the skill in presenting offers quickly is a great way to *smoke out a seller's motivation level.* All you are trying to do is bring the seller to the table to talk it over and see if you can work together. What happens if you only get one out of every twenty-five offers but that one makes you $10,000, $20,000, $30,000? Would that make you happy? Be prepared to receive a lot of "No, thanks" to your written offers, but do not be downhearted. You're looking for diamonds, not semiprecious gems. Which would you rather have, one deal that makes you $25,000 or five that make you $5,000 each? You're not looking to buy every property you make an offer on, as in retail real estate. *You're looking for the wholesale diamond.*

Get Real!
Present written offers sight unseen, using a fax or e-mail

Written offers can be presented quickly by fax or e-mail. Our government agreed several years ago that electronic signatures would be considered binding. However, a contract is not formalized until there is a transfer of "good and valuable consideration," which would be the deposit. Better yet, I'll be showing you how to be sure to write into your agreement a way to get out of it.

Get Real!
Make your offer good for only the next thirty-six hours

Shortening the deadline forces the other party to respond quickly to your offer. Make the offer good for only thirty-six hours. This creates urgency and makes sure the seller doesn't sit on the offer. If you're working with an agent, he or she must be flexible and adjust his or her way of doing business to accommodate your approach. This is highly out of the ordinary for agents, and the reason they must see ahead of time what they are going to get out of it.

The agent also must be reassured that you're real about following through with your intentions. The agent's managing broker may not be supportive and/or knowledgeable about wholesale buying techniques and, in turn, may not be excited about an agent spending time doing this. Be sensitive to these issues and search for an agent who does understand what you are doing and why he or she should jump at the opportunity to work with you.

Once you've presented the offer and reached an agreement, you're at first base. *You got control by taking it off the market.* That's all you wanted to do for now. Get control to buy time to evaluate all the factors involved.

Get Real!
Control the paperwork

If you are working with a real estate agent, he or she probably already has a "standard" contract the agent prefers using or is required to use by his or her managing broker. This standard or "board certified" contract that local agencies like to use is not required by law for all real estate transactions. Agents prefer using it because they are already familiar with it, which makes their job easier, and because it generally protects the interests of their client—the seller. Your goal is to get to the point where you use exclusively your own *standard* contract and play the game in your ballpark. *You want to control the paperwork.* Your "standard" contract should be written to protect the interests of you, the buyer.

Get Real!

Make more money in less time by using the best tools available

The *American Financial Education Network* provides easy-to-use software that has all the documents a professional investor needs: buyer agreement, seller agreement, lease/option, equity sharing, agreement for deed, assignment of contract, and many others. This powerful software system puts you in the category of professionals. One of the best investments I ever made was acquiring the right software to automate my needs. It makes me more money in less time. I've had attorneys and accountants use this software for their own investing as well as for use in their practices. It is a timesaving tool you'll eventually want to be sure to have. See GetRealMoney.com\tools.

At this point, your goal is twofold. First, take the property off the market; second, make sure to protect yourself. Once you reach an initial agreement with a seller, the property can't legally be sold to someone else without your permission. That's the idea. If it's a great opportunity, you can bet there may be someone on your heels who is just as smart. Get the property off the market and give yourself more time to talk to your potential investment partners, inspect the property, and make a final buying decision.

Get Real!
The Safety Net Strategy™

Protecting yourself is important. That's one reason why I want you to control the paperwork. You must *put in your document a way to get out.* By doing so, you have time to gather all the necessary details and make a good buying decision rather than a rush decision. There are several ways to protect yourself. I like inserting a special clause which begins with the words "subject to."

"Subject to buyer's partners' approval"—this is a safety net and gives you the right to back out if you want to. This creates a protection that says the terms and conditions of this contract are subject to your partners' approval. Who are your partners, and how long will it be before they approve? What happens if they don't? Good questions! This is a highly open-ended wording that *protects you* and is to your advantage—the ball is in your ballpark. That's the name of the game. Up until this point in your life, everyone has expected you to use paperwork created by his or her attorney, right?

In the last few years, have you signed any important documents? Whose attorney drew it up, and whom was it protecting? You get the idea. It's a shrewd world out there, and I'm teaching you to play hardball the way it is played. People with money are no dummies, and we didn't get there playing softball! At this point, all you are trying to do is *take the property off the market* to get the facts in front of you in an organized fashion. We'll talk about the ethical considerations of this in just a moment. For those of you who want to find out other excellent real estate contract strategies that can make you significant money, visit www.GetRealMoney.com. The next step is to make a decision to buy or to properly "back out." Notice, at this point in the game you have located a potential diamond and tied it up so no one else can take it away.

Get Real!

Hire a professional property inspector before you buy

Now is the time to do your own inspection. There are two inspections that must be completed—a financial inspection and a physical inspection. It is entirely possible for you to have secured an *equitable interest* in the property without having yet seen it yourself. That's what is referred to as securing a contract to purchase the property "sight unseen." Now is the time to visit the property for a quick physical inspection. At this point, this is not the formal property inspection. You will hire a professional to do that at the right time. You are going to get an overall look at the property yourself. Your goal is to determine basics, such as what work obviously must be done, curb appeal, anything major you didn't expect (the house next door is burned down), etc. You want to roughly calculate the costs of putting the property into resalable or rental condition. You will hire an expert to do a formal property inspection for you once you open escrow (closing procedures begin). A professional inspection costs between $250 and $350, depending on how many units the property has and the pricing you've worked out.

I have found that once you develop some experience, you can quickly estimate a fix-up cost within a 10 percent range of the cost of what it is going to take, so leave room for error. Don't expect or trust yourself to be the professional property inspector. There's more to inspections than most people understand. Always hire a professional property inspector.

Get Real!

Cash Back at Closing Strategy

Complete a *preliminary inspection report* detailing the work that must be done. This document can be used for two purposes: to negotiate a discount or to get money back at closing. By using a formal document called an inspection report, you now have something real to go back to the seller with and the *tool* to negotiate with. A well done inspection report details what items need repair, attention, or replacing. It also states a total cost and provides a contractor's estimate. That way it's not your estimate; it's a contractor's. Negotiating again, after you have the property under contract, may result in the seller either lowering the price or crediting back money to the buyer at closing for necessary repairs.

Get Real!
Financial Inspection Strategy™

The next step is in knowing the *real* numbers and doing a *financial inspection*. This is called a *cash flow analysis,* or a real estate business plan, as I like to call it. The financial inspection is just as important as a physical inspection if you're planning on holding the property for rental purposes. Never buy a piece of real estate you plan to hold unless this is done properly. It is based on expected rents (income) and a history of documented expenses. The equation works like this, but believe me, there is much more to it. This is simplified to help you get the point:

$$\begin{array}{ll} \text{GI} & \text{gross income} \\ -\text{OE} & \text{operating expenses} \\ \hline \text{NOI} & \text{net operating income} \end{array}$$

The *Get Real! Diamond Mining System* also includes an entire cash flow analysis software tool to help you do this properly, saving you thousands of dollars and many hours of time. The only expense left to be taken in this example is the mortgage payment. This expense fluctuates based on how you structured the financing. Visit www.GetRealMoney.com and you will find a complete Cash Flow Analysis Worksheet you can follow, as well as suggested approaches to structuring the financing.

Get Real!

Hold only property that has a minimum positive cash flow of $150 per month

Your goal when you buy and hold real estate is—positive cash flow. Notice the word *positive*. I have had many students at my *Get Real! Money Seminars* who already own real estate and yet never really did an accurate cash flow analysis. They did their best, but this is something you can't just wing and hope for the best. Every investor must know and have confidence in doing a cash flow analysis. That's what we teach them. You save yourself lots of headaches by knowing what mistakes not to make.

My recommendation for all my students is to buy and hold only property with a minimum positive cash flow of $150 per month. That's including only having 10 percent of your own money into the transaction. The more money you put into it, the more positive the cash flow should be. Your goal, however, is to learn to keep your money in your pocket and to use OPM (other people's money).

Get Real!

Use real estate to leverage other people's money

When we finance real estate, we are really having a partner put up the money. This is financial leverage. Generally, you want to leverage the property as much as possible, based on your long-term plan. For example, you may put a ten-year plan in place that yields $5,000 per month positive cash flow. So you calculate the financing to make a ten-year payoff work. You begin by starting with a plan and then make the project *fit the plan* rather than the other way around. This way you stay focused on what you need to do to make transactions work.

Get Real!
Make money on the way in—and on the way out

Here's the fast and easy rule: *I'm making money the day I sign the contract.* You're not hoping that we have miracle appreciation or that Wal-Mart goes in next door. You calculate the deal as it stands today. I suggest a conservative approach to investing that will factor in a modest 3 percent appreciation in value and rents. I suggest that you not bet on unreliable profit potential, such as new sewers going in or rezoning to commercial or future development, unless you are seasoned and understand these factors. As mentioned earlier, leave that to others. There's plenty of room for you doing it conservatively.

Instead, I suggest that you contract a property that you know you can buy at a significant discount from day one. It's not uncommon to find property that you purchase for 20 to 50 percent discounts—people do it every day of the week. All you need is one or two of those a year to make a huge impact on your financial well-being. I've worked with many families who have increased their financial net worth by as much as $25,000 in one transaction. Ask yourself, how long would it take the average family to save $25,000? Probably 25,000 years! You can do that in real estate in one deal!

Get Real!
Flip for Quick Cash Strategy

If your plan is to make money quickly by *flipping* the deal, your interest is in getting an excellent price. For example, if you were to get a $75,000 house under contract for $50,000 and you calculated it would take about $10,000 to close on it and fix it up, you would now have $60,000 into it. If you were to sell it slightly discounted at $70,000, you would have made a nice $10,000 profit. By the way, I know that my readers in San Francisco, Seattle, and New York, to name a few places, are thinking, "Where in the world do you buy a house for

$75,000?" Well, not in your neighborhood, at least not any-more. But you'd be amazed to know that all over the United States there are millions of properties still available for well under $75,000. The principle is what I want you to capture, and yes, the numbers must always work. I've taught several hundred real estate investment seminars all over the United States, and I know that property values differ everywhere I go, but the principles remain the same. You must get a $400,000 property for $325,000 and sell it for $350,000 to make a profit in a place like San Francisco (which, by the way, is only a three-bed, two-bath, 1,300-square-foot ranch). I can remember when you could buy houses on the side of the hill in Seattle for $80,000 to $100,000, and it wasn't that long ago! Real estate has appreciated tremendously in some places.

Get Real!

Get a great deal and give a new buyer a good deal

The rule of flipping is this: *I've got to get a great deal and give somebody a good deal.* For example:

$150,000	Fair market value of property
$120,000	Contract purchase price (great deal)
$140,000	Resell/flip price (good deal)
$20,000	**Profit**

Be sure the transaction fits your cookie-cutter model. And make sure you follow through to buy it only if it fits your plan. That's how you make your decision to buy or not to buy. Now, what happens if you've gotten the property under contract and you decide, for some reason, not to buy?

Get Real!

Exercise your right to rescind your offer when necessary

You exercise your *right* secured in your agreement to not buy the property. The best way to do this is in written form, saying that you are exercising your right to let the other party out of the agreement, thereby formally releasing him or her from any obligation. Yes, there is an ethical consideration here that you must be aware of. Suppose your contract is accepted and it read, "Subject to buyer's partners' approval." This is open-ended with no time limitation stated (which you can negotiate if the seller objects at the time of the offer).

Get Real!
Always do what's right

I find that the best way to do business is by having a predetermined set of standards by which to operate. One of my standards is to *always do what's right*. Another is, do to others as you would have them do to you. I feel it's entirely reasonable to exercise your right to not buy a property in most situations—under two conditions.

Let's assume the seller is highly motivated, because he's four months behind in his mortgage payments, and he's ill and out of work. You come along and provide a "solution" to one of his problems. You'll stop the foreclosure, make up his back payments, pay his penalties, and give him an additional $5,000 above and beyond. I would clearly say to the seller at the time he signs the contract, "Mr. Seller, I look forward to seeing if I can help you in this situation. However, one thing I want you to be aware of is that I must put some details in place. I must talk with my partner and look closely at your home. This will take several days. I don't want you to get too excited just yet, because I may choose not to go through with this. Today is Saturday, and I will let you know for sure by Tuesday at 5 p.m. Does that seem reasonable to you?"

You've made a point of keeping his expectations in perspective until you are absolutely sure you will follow through. This is *reasonable* in this situation, the *right thing to do*, and the way I would want to be treated. *Simple, straightforward, up-*

front, honest, and direct.

Now let's use another example. Suppose the seller is motivated and agrees to sell you one of his or her forty properties. This is a different story, because he is seasoned and knows what to expect. If I were to come back ten days later and exercise my right not to purchase the property, it's not devastating to the seller. Always consider with whom you are dealing. Never forget that good business is still about real people just like you. Treat them right, even if it costs you. Walk away if someone tries to hurt you. Learn the lesson and move on. It will happen. Just stay away and avoid getting into any legal conflicts. Many attorneys make a living creating havoc for people, when in many of these cases reasonable people can work things out without a third party.

Get Real!
Put the details in place last

Next you must put details in place—little items like where the money is going to come from. Notice how this was left until the last step. There's a reason for this. You see, this is where most people would stop, throw up their hands, and say, "I can't do it. I don't have enough money; I don't have credit." Well, that may all be true—unless you've learned to operate differently. You've got to begin to see the situation from another point of view.

Get Real!
Work from the perspective of abundance versus lack

I want you to view yourself from a perspective of "abundance" versus "lack." It's time to realize what you bring to the table in terms of skill, knowledge, sweat equity, and courage. You may not have the money or the credit, but whatever you may not have, somebody does. Many times another person may not have the specialized knowledge or the time that you do. Might this be a potential working arrangement? That's the idea; you've got to get the ball rolling somehow. Sure, it would be great if you had all the money in the world to just buy property for all cash and figure out how to finance it long term later. It would be great to have impeccable credit and all the time in the world, but you might not, and that's reality. Look at the bright side and the assets you are bringing to the table. There are people who need you. Millions of investors have gotten clobbered in the stock market over the last several years and are in need of a stable and secure place to invest money, such as real estate. People like to invest in assets they can touch and see.

Get Real!

Form strategic alliances based on the knowledge, skills, drive, and determination you bring to the table

Here's a good opportunity to use OPM and OPC. OPM is other people's money, and OPC is other people's credit. Form strategic alliances based on the knowledge, skills, drive, and determination you bring to the table. Find a partner you enjoy working with, whom you know you can trust, and reach an agreement. Remember, the vast majority of people are scared of investing, and have money in savings accounts or certificates of deposit (CDs). You have an opportunity that can potentially yield them 25 percent, 50 percent, or higher. They would be stupid not to seriously consider a well-presented offer to partner in a good real estate deal. There are many people who have great credit, but might not have the time or specialized knowledge it takes to find a good deal. An excellent strategy here is an equity-sharing agreement, whereby one partner puts up the money and the credit for a share of the profit. See www.GetRealMoney.com under Real Estate for more details on equity sharing.

Get Real!

Interview and choose a good title company to handle your details

You also need the assistance of a title company or closing agent to help put details in place. In some areas of the country, they are called title companies; in other areas, they are known as escrow agents. It is worth your time interviewing several. Find one you genuinely like on a personal level. Look at how the agent keeps his or her office. Does it look like a tornado just walked in? If so, that's the way the agent probably will handle clients' files—not good. Or, is he well organized? Does she return calls promptly? Does he provide good service?

You are hiring these people for their administrative and legal expertise as well as their level of service. They all charge about the same, and you may be working with them on a regular basis. Find someone you really like and respect. The title company or closing/escrow agent handles the paperwork and most legal matters. He or she assists you in putting the necessary steps in place to close the transaction.

The closing agent begins by "opening escrow," which means creating a working file beginning with a closing date. He or she typically begins by having the title researched and an abstract completed to discover any and all liens on the property and if there are any unknown restrictions you must be aware of. The agent does this to be sure the title is insurable. He or she sells you the necessary title insurance. This is one of the agent's profit centers.

Title agents are great for answering questions and giving general advice. If they are attorneys, you can rely on them for their legal *opinions*. That's what they are paid for. They are hired to represent your interests in the transaction. A good title agent is an important player on your team. Invest the time necessary to develop a solid long-term relationship with your title agent.

Now that you've closed on the property, what do you do? What you do with the property depends on your plan. Are you going to fix it up for resale, or are you going to hold it for rent? Either way, your goal is to move fast, because time is money, and every day you hold a property that is either not rented or sitting unsold increases your holding costs, cutting into your overall profits. Make sure you are prepared to take fast action the day you close on the property.

There are dozens of strategies you could implement here. At www.GetRealMoney.com, you'll discover the lease option, professional property management strategies, assignment of contract strategy, and so on. Take the time and review these strategies, and get busy with the ones best for your situation. Before we end this chapter, I want to pull it all together and show you the power of what I have been teaching you. Would you be able to survive if you had $1 million in an investment account? Let me show you how to do just that and at the same time generate an income of more than $5,000 per month from that account.

Get Real!
The $1,000,000 Investment Account Strategy™

Suppose you were to begin your investment portfolio of real estate by purchasing $1 million worth of real estate as fast as you can using no money down. Let's assume that you use the buy-and-hold strategy and that the property provides you a positive cash flow of $1,000 per month after all expenses, which would be reasonable. As time passes, the mortgages will be paid off. In fact, you could accelerate the payoff by adding additional principal payments, which gives you your $1 million investment account sooner rather than later. Let's assume for this example that you pay off the property in twenty years rather than thirty.

Over time the property will appreciate in value at approximately the cost of living (3 percent). As the property appreciates

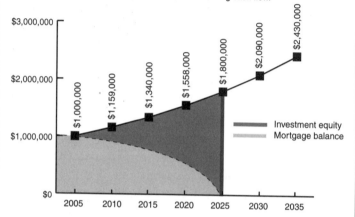

GetRealMoney.com
$1,000,000 Investment Account Strategy™

In the year 2025, $1,800,000 will hold the same value as $1,000,000 did in 2005. Your real estate mortgages will be completely paid off providing you with a large, permanent, and recurring cash flow.

Investment equity
Mortgage balance

*Calculations are based on the assumption that the cost of living will increase approximately 3% annually on average as they have done so historically over the past 100 years in the United States. Real estate values have also appreciated approximately 3% annually on average throughout the United States over the past 100 years.

© 2005 New Discovery Media Corporation

in value, it will some day be worth $1.34 million, $1.8 million, etc. Meanwhile, the cost of living rises at almost exactly the same rate as the value of the property appreciates (3 percent) leaving you with the same buying power that the $1 million holds today—but now the property is completely paid for. You no longer have mortgage payments, and the positive cash flow has gone through the roof ($5,000 to $8,000 per month). Remember, rents also increase with the cost of living. So the same property that you at one time rented for $500 per unit will eventually be renting for $800, then $1,000. Think for just a minute what you have accomplished by putting this one strategy in place—a $1 million investment account!

Can you stop working with a $5,000 to $8,000 per month

positive cash flow? Will you have a *permanent recurring income* that will last your lifetime and beyond? Will you have a *safety hedge* in case you lose your job or your other business goes belly up? Does this shield you from the rise in the cost of living and the shrinking dollar? Yes, yes, yes!

Take a moment to study the $1,000,000 Investment Account Strategy chart. This will give you an excellent picture of what we have been discussing.

Get Real!
Free College Education Strategy™

One of the best strategies for paying for a child's college education is to hire your college-age child to be your investment property manager of the apartment he or she is living in while going to school. This will make a portion of the money you'll be providing him or her earned income rather than a freebie. This converts non-tax deductible expenses into a 100 percent tax deduction.

For example, as a parent you have enormous outflows of money going toward sending your child to college—housing, food, tuition, books, and travel. Suppose that child is employed by you as manager of your investment property. You can now elect to provide your manager housing, and perhaps pay for the cost of the education as it relates to helping him manage the property, as well as your travel for property inspections from time to time. Your manager must also visit you for occasional business meetings. Meanwhile, the property is appreciating in value and your child is learning real-life responsibility. Also, your investment property won't become the Animal House with him or her as the property manager—at least we hope not! When he is ready to move on, you now have an investment that has appreciated, the mortgage has been paid down, and the property will be easy to sell to the next parent, especially by showing that person what you have accomplished. Rather than an education bill, you have a nice gain in property value to help pay for your child's education, as well as a child who has a skill that can make him or her wealthy! Also, don't miss the fact that a portion of the education that your child is receiving could potentially be deductible as either a direct expense necessary for operating a property management business or as an employee benefit for your employee (child). This would depend on how you structure your arrangement with your child, and I suggest you speak with a qualified tax advisor about this scenario.

Get Real!

Keep developing your specialized knowledge in real estate by committing to the long-term education process

Real estate is a fascinating investment. It is by far the fastest way to generate large lump sums of money, as well as one of the only investments where you can earn investment cash-on-cash returns well over 100 percent. I suggest that you commit to the long-term process of getting the real knowledge your need to become a confident real estate investor. You will find much more help at www.GetRealMoney.com.

Get Real!

Real estate is the safest, most lucrative, and most flexible investment for amateur and advanced investors alike who know what they are doing

Real estate is a fascinating investment and, by far, one of the only investments where you can generate large lump sums of money. It is one of the only investments where you can earn cash-on-cash returns well over 100 percent.

Real estate provides tremendous flexibility in terms of building a portfolio of property producing recurring income or buying and selling for a quicker profit. I suggest that you commit to the long-term process of getting the knowledge you need to become a confident real estate investor.

Your New Beginning

Congratulations! You've come a long way since you started reading *Get Real! Money*! You now know more than what 99 percent of Americans know when it comes to *how money really works and how to get yours*. Now's the time to go *Get Real! Money* and apply the *7 Minute Secret*—daily.

Commit yourself right now to the *7 Minute Secret*. Apply yourself every day—no days off, seven minutes a day for the next ten days then twenty, then forty. Stay with it for one year. You will look back 365 days from now and be amazed at how far you have come and what you have achieved. Keep your learning momentum, and take action and apply what you have learned seven minutes a day.

I want to personally thank you for reading this book. It truly has been my privilege to share my *Get Real! Strategies* with you and I sincerely wish you the best of success, not only with money, but with life. I look forward to some day soon either speaking with you on one of our special telephone conferences, or personally meeting you at one of my *Get Real! Money Seminars*.

Feel free to write to me and my staff, telling us what you think about what you have learned. The best way to share your thoughts with us is through www.GetRealMoney.com\survey. You'll find a survey, which will provide us with feedback, and we'll send you an additional BONUS for taking the time to participate in the survey. Please keep us informed on how you are progressing. We will always do our best to respond.

To your success,
Jim Guarino

Get Real!
MONEY SERIES™

UPCOMING *Get Real!* TITLES
2005–2007

Get Real! MONEY for Women

Safely Create a Secure Financial Future in Just 7 Minutes a Day

How to proactively deal with the pressures of earning enough and how to confidently take charge of your financial future with or without the support of a partner.

Get Real! MONEY Self-Employed

Secrets to Safe and Successful Self-Employment 7 Minutes a Day

How to safely be self-employed either part-time or full-time. Learn how to avoid costly mistakes. Discover secrets that only seasoned entrepreneurs know and learn how to profit from their mistakes.

Get Real! MONEY Real Estate

Secrets to Safe and Successful Investing 7 Minutes a Day

How to safely invest in real estate part-time. Proven and powerful money-making strategies for beginners as well as advanced investors. Use the *Get Real! Diamond Mining System*™ for finding profitable opportunities that will make serious money. Learn the secrets to protect yourself financially using real estate.

Get Real! MONEY for People Who Want God's Best

How to Make, Save and Invest Money 7 Minutes a Day

How to make *real* money, save *real* money, and invest *real* money with confidence in a way that will honor and please your Creator.

★ ★ ★ ★ ★
American Financial
EDUCATION NETWORK

JIM GUARINO is founder and president of the *American Financial Education Network* (AFEN), a worldwide alliance of trusted companies providing quality resources, tools, and education for AFEN members' success. Since 1990 Jim has been instrumental in bringing valuable financial, business, and personal development education and support to thousands of individuals, businesses, and corporations.

American Financial Education Network presents live educational events called *Get Real! Money Seminars*. Find out how you can attend. Visit *www.AFEN.org*.

Here's what everybody's saying about

Makes It Easy . . .

"Wow! Jim really made money so easy to understand. Thank you, Jim!"
—Melea, homemaker, AR

"He delivers the information clearly, and concisely. Also, his sense of humor and patience 'make it easy' and pleasant for me to understand." —Doris, minister, CA

"Made it easy to understand." —Diane, self-employed

"…easy to understand and informative. I never fell asleep once." —Lisa, law enforcement, SC

Inspiring and Motivating . . .

"I will succeed in all my expectations from this wealth of information." —Steve, OR

"I feel enthused and empowered now to 'take the next step' toward my financial freedom and 'redesigning' the way I want to live life. Thank you, Jim"! —Elizabeth, businesswoman, MI

"…opened my eyes to the reality that I am worthy to dream…" —Karen, self-employed, WA

"Jim helped me refocus and regain my VISION for my life! This has been a Godsend!"
—Gerardo, evangelist, producer/recording artist, TX

"I have found myself truly inspired…thanks for sincerely touching my life."
—Dave, law enforcement, WA

"It's opened up new areas of possibilities for me personally and professionally."
—Richard, WA

"Truly one of the most interesting and motivational speakers I have had the pleasure of learning from. Jim is such a polished professional—I'm proud to have been in his company…" —Vickie, radio broadcasting executive, FL

The Best of the Best . . .

"I've been attending seminars for years. What you have done is take some of the most important segments of these seminars and package them in one weekend. I can't wait to get my three boys to one of your next seminars for this road map of financial freedom of life! Thanks so much." —Paul, real estate broker, TN

"In my opinion, Jim is one of the best in the field. I am truly blessed to have met this man."
—Mike, electrician, TN

"…the best I've ever attended." —Rose Marie, entrepreneur, WA

"Jim is the best presenter we have had the good fortune to hear and get to know…"
—Bette, Realtor, IN

"Jim is the best speaker and teacher I have heard." —William, controller, IN

"Jim's presentation and communication skills are beyond excellence!"
—Eddie, real estate broker, TX

"I've been to many seminars…I put Jim on the top." —Elizabeth, sales and marketing, MO

"After building a real estate portfolio of over $8 million in value, I find the most valuable portfolio I own is my personal education. Thanks again, Jim."
—Allen, real estate developer-investor, SC

"Jim is top rated." —Rick, homebuilder, VA

Life Changing . . .

"I feel Jim is a turning point in my life that is long over due." —Christine, registered massage therapist, TX

"This was truly a life-changing experience. The most helpful and informative class I have ever attended." —Lionel, personal banker, WV

"He captivates one's attention based on factual information coupled with dynamic approaches to enrich one's financial picture now and for the future."
—Doris, interior designer, VA

"I know God sent you my way." —McKenzie, supervisor, VA

Personable, Down-to-Earth . . .

"I appreciate your kind words of encouragement." —Jack, seventy-five-year-old general contractor, CA

"I was able to refocus my investing activities." —Richard, finance manager, CA

"He really eased some of my fears…" —Jasper/educator

"Extremely friendly and patient!" —L.B., investor, MI

"Jim's teaching style is very personable and thorough." —Loretta, sales representative, ME

"I appreciate your honesty and family values." —Ken, business owner, TX

"I would challenge you to find someone as personable and apt to learn this info from as Jim."
—Fred, businessman, SC

"It was a once-in-a-lifetime, heartfelt experience to this point in my life. You rarely find such an up-front speaker who seems to genuinely share and feel for others."
—Eugene, real estate broker-investor, MO

Tremendous Value . . .

"He knows how to make money and how to teach his students to do the same."
—Gilmer, retired colonel, U.S. Army, GA

"Pulls no punches, tells it like it is …" —Alrick, engineer, OH

"…currently my net worth is almost $2 million. I came to improve my cash position…"
—Michael, investor-entrepreneur, CA

"This seminar was an excellent investment and was a great experience working and learning from Jim." —Wayne, real estate investor, AR

Superb . . .

"He is well versed on all subject matter he delivers." —Ronald, correctional lieutenant, AR

"…very clear and exciting." —Keith, financial planner, OH

"His method of teaching was superb!" —Julie, college professor, SC

"Right to the point." —Barrie, real estate investor-entrepreneur, SC

"This is for anyone wanting to be more financially secure not only for themselves but for their family." —Loretta, real estate investor, AR

"Lots of substance professionally presented…" —Byron, retired insurance agent, MI

Highly Recommend . . .

"We would highly recommend you to our family, friends, and business associates."
—Dawn, businesswoman, GA

"We have listened to numerous seminars across the country and across the globe; Jim is the best by far…" —Giancarlo, business owner, SC

"Jim helped give us points that would have taken years of experience to have learned on our own. We would certainly attend another seminar if he is back in our area and would recommend him with high compliments." —Diana and Edward, sales, VA

"I would recommend Jim to speak for any company…" —Edward, businessman-investor, KS

JIM GUARINO

Keynote Speaker / Seminar Leader

Jim is an entrepreneur, master trainer, and one of the top professional speakers in the United States. Jim's speeches and seminars are tailored for each audience. He is *"inspiring, entertaining, down-to-earth, and highly motivating"* and has given more than 1,000 speeches/seminars over the past fifteen years. Jim has worked with tens of thousands of individuals, and hundreds of businesses and corporations.

His topics include:

- Get Real! Money:
  Get Real! Game Plan for Success

- Get Real! Motivated:
  Peak Performance Mastery

- Get Real! Money:
  Sales and Marketing

- Get Real! Free Enterprise:
  Business Success

Jim will carefully customize his keynote speech or seminar for your audience to meet your specific needs. Find out if Jim is available for your next meeting or conference. Contact Jim at www.GetRealMoney.com or phone New Discovery Media Corporation at 800-780-0355.

NEW
DISCOVERY™
MEDIA CORPORATION

BONUS SECTION

7 Minute Action Steps

Action Step 1

Commit right now and schedule your 7 Minutes a Day. Choose the same time each day for the next twenty-one days. Do it now!

Action Step 2

Sign up for your FREE! Special Gift Subscription to *TheMoneyExpert* newsletter and Special Gift Reports if you haven't yet. This will help you stay motivated and keep you on track to reaching your goals.

Action Step 3

Join us for special teleconferences as often as you can. You will learn something each time you listen in.

Action Step 4

Read this book over again! Let it sink in, and create for yourself a list of action plans for your new financial future.

7 Minute Action Steps

_____

_____

_____

_____

_____

_____

_____

_____

_____

_____

_____

_____

_____

_____

_____

_____

7 Minute Action Steps

_____

_____

_____

_____

_____

_____

_____

_____

_____

_____

_____

_____

_____

_____

_____

_____